BROKEN BONDS
to CONNECTION

PRACTICAL AND SPIRITUAL GUIDANCE
FOR FAMILIES OF THE INCARCERATED

HEIDI J. SHELDON

Disclaimer

This book is a memoir reflecting the author's personal experiences and perspective as the parent of an incarcerated adult child. It also includes guidance and insights based on the author's journey. The content is provided for informational and support purposes only and is not a substitute for professional, legal, or medical advice. Readers should seek advice from qualified professionals regarding their own circumstances.

Certain names, identifying details, and events have been changed or omitted to protect the privacy of individuals mentioned. While the events described are true to the author's experience, some details may have been condensed or altered for clarity and confidentiality.

The author and publisher disclaim any liability for actions taken or not taken based on the content of this book.

Copyright © 2025 by Heidi J. Sheldon
Editor: Krystal Hille
Published by: Hille House Publishing

ISBN: 978-1-7641985-8-5 (Paperback)
ISBN: 978-1-7641985-9-2 (E-book)

All Rights Reserved

Apart from any fair dealing for the purpose of research or private study, criticism, or review, as permitted under the Copyright, Designs, and Patents Act 1988, this publication may only be reproduced, stored, or transmitted in any form or by any means with the prior permission in writing of the copyright owner, or in the case of the reprographic reproduction, in accordance with the terms of licensees issued by the Copyright Licensing Agency. Enquiries concerning reproduction outside those terms should be sent to the publisher.

Dedication

To my son, Takodah—

Your journey reminds me every day of the mercy of God. As the song says, "I'm living proof of what the mercy of God can do. Now I'm alive to tell the story, how I've overcome."

We are alive to tell the story together, because His mercy covered us both.

contents

Acknowledgements	VII
INTRODUCTION	IX
1. Connection	1
2. Shock	13
3. What You Need to Know Once In Jail	25
4. A New Jail, A New Reality	35
5. Our Faith Walk	45
6. The Weight We Carry	59
7. Early Transfer	69
8. Sentencing	77
9. The Hit	87
10. The New Normal and One Hiccup	97
Epilogue: A Word to You	103
Scripture and References	105

Acknowledgements

There are many people who have helped me through this journey, and I am deeply grateful to each of you.

To my husband: you have been my solid rock. From calling the detective, to offering gentle guidance, to simply listening to my fears—you have walked this road with me. Thank you for supporting me while I spent hours away visiting my son and for allowing me to grow in my faith.

To the Beyond Walls support group through Alaska Correctional Ministries: your compassion has been without comparison. Thank you to Chaplain Rudy, Chaplain Bryan, and all those who serve families and incarcerated loved ones. Your presence has been a lifeline to me and to so many others.

To my mom: how can I possibly thank you enough? You have always been my greatest cheerleader, even when you lived 3,000 miles away. Thank you for loving me and your grandchildren so deeply. Both Takodah and his sister have been shaped by your love, your adventures with them in New England, and your faithful support in Alaska.

To my dear daughter: you have carried more than most your age should bear—from being your brother's confidant to receiving the news of his arrest while away at college. I hope you know how deeply you are loved and how important you are to me.

To Krystal of Hille House Publishing: we met through Darren Hardy's Hero's Journey program, and now you have shepherded me through the publishing of this book. Thank you for your hours of guidance, for keeping me on track, and for helping me uncover the thread of connection that runs through my story—the ultimate connection with God.

To the women friends I've gained along this journey: growing up, I never had close women friends. But through this season, God has brought into my life the most wonderful sisters in Christ. None of us chose to have our sons incarcerated, yet our love and compassion for one another have sustained me many nights. Thank you.

And to my son, Takodah: without you, God's glory would not have shone so brightly in my life. Your faith and incredible growth have shown me God's true grace. Through your journey, I found my acceptance of Jesus Christ. I celebrate our shared faith and especially our baptism on the same day, November 5. I cannot wait to see all the works God will do through you, inside and outside of prison. I love you.

INTRODUCTION

What is it like to have an incarcerated child?

Have you ever said, "Thank God he has been arrested, I know he is alive?"
I have.

Have you ever been scrolling on Facebook and found out your child is a person of interest?
I have.

Because one died and another was injured?
I have.

I never imagined I'd be navigating the criminal justice system. I had never visited anyone in prison before. But here I am, three years later, still learning.

You may feel guilt, fear, shame, the desire to isolate yourself from everyone, searching for answers, shock, and disbelief. I've felt them all since the beginning, and even now in 2025.

You may be like me and never thought you would ever have this title. Even if this isn't your first experience, you may still feel these emotions deeply. My son was no saint before he was arrested. I knew he had a stack of speeding tickets, and recently learned he was one speeding ticket away from having a suspended license! But I never thought I'd be visiting him in jail.

At our Beyond Walls support group (a group for friends and family of incarcerated individuals), the chaplain often says, "We don't go to school for this." And he's right. If the state corrections website had a dedicated link for family support of inmates—like they do for victims—my journey might have been far less stressful. A simple list of local support groups, guidance on essential paperwork like a state power of attorney (rather than the prison-supplied version), and key advice—such as always accepting help from a public defender—would have made a world of difference.

Instead, I had to piece things together on my own, asking questions wherever I could—first to the police officers, then family members, jail employees, the state corrections website, our public defender, and, most importantly, other mothers walking this same path. Through it all, my local support group became a lifeline, reminding me that while we don't go to school for this, we don't have to navigate it alone.

If you are in the early stages of your journey with an incarcerated child, let me provide some hope and tell you a recent story to illustrate the growth you will go through.

I was expecting his call. My friend, another mom on this same path, had told her son to tell my son to call me. He had been accepted into an Undergraduate School of Bible and Theology.

"Hello," I said after being told, "You can begin the call" from the auto Securus voice (don't worry—I'll tell you all about the phone system that sometimes works).

"Hi Mom," he responded with hope in his voice.

"I have your login information. I've changed your password," I said.

"Is there anything about scholarships?" he asked.

"No," I replied.

"I have to go," he said in a rush. Click!

I stared at the phone for a moment, my stomach clenching out of habit. But this time, the anxiety quickly loosened its grip. *Probably another lockdown*, I thought. I've learned not to panic over every dropped call. But that shift didn't happen overnight.

In the beginning, I wouldn't have imagined writing a book like this. I didn't think I had a story worth sharing. Mine wasn't dramatic or headline-worthy. Just a quiet, messy life with mistakes, growth, and the ache of trying to love well. I used to think of it as boring—vanilla. But I've learned that God uses all kinds of stories. Especially the quiet ones. The ones told by tired mothers, who are learning how to fight for their children, and finding hope in the process.

I now know my "ordinary" story is exactly what someone else might need to hear, what *you* might need to hear.

Three years ago, though, it would have been a different story. My stomach would've stayed knotted for hours, waiting anxiously for his next call. I was drowning in fear back then—fear of the unknown, fear of what his future held, and fear of what it meant for me as his mom.

It's been three years of this back-and-forth. Years of calls that sometimes end too quickly. Times not recognizing the phone number because all of a sudden, he had been moved to a different facility. Years of different visitation rooms, navigating rules, and adjusting to a world I never thought I'd be part of. And in March 2025, he was sentenced, and we have begun a new norm.

You Are Not Alone

You are not alone. The bridge to hope lies in moving from isolation to connection—first with others who understand, and ultimately with God.

In fact, you are far from alone. In 2022, the United States had 1.23 million incarcerated individuals. In Alaska alone, where I live, there were 4,778. Behind each of those numbers are families—parents, siblings, spouses—facing the same shock and loss I did. This is not just my story or my son's story; it's a story shared by countless families across the country.

Connection is what transforms despair into hope. When we're isolated, our pain feels heavier, our fears louder, and our struggles insurmountable. But when we reach out—when we find others who have walked this road—we discover strength we never knew we had. Their stories become lifelines, reminding us that survival is possible, that healing can happen, and that even in the darkest moments, there is a way forward.

As we open ourselves to others, we also open the door for God to work in our lives. He meets us in our brokenness, drawing near to the weary and the wounded. As Psalm 34:18 reminds us, "The Lord is close to the brokenhearted and saves those who are crushed in spirit." [1]

When my world first flipped upside down, I felt lost, afraid, and completely unprepared. I'll never forget the shock of seeing my son during that first visitation—one hand cuffed to a bar, cradling the phone with the other. My mind screamed, *How did we get here?*

Maybe you've asked yourself the same question. Maybe, like me, you've faced the overwhelming guilt that only a parent can feel. But I want you to know there's hope.

This book is here to guide you through the pain, the confusion, and the guilt. I'll share what I've learned—about navigating this unfamiliar system, about rebuilding connections, and about finding healing and faith along the way.

> *"For I know the plans I have for you,"* declares the Lord, *"plans to prosper you and not to harm you, plans to give you hope and a future."*
> —Jeremiah 29:11 (NIV)[2]

As I reflect on my journey from hearing about the arrest to the final sentencing, I know the truthfulness of this verse. But I didn't have this faith when it all began. I wasn't a practicing Christian. I had no idea that, through the hardest season of my life, I'd find Jesus as my Savior. It's been a slow process—three years of mini-transformations—but the faith I've gained has brought me hope. And that hope has helped me find strength I didn't know I had.

I wrote this book to walk with you through the storm. Together, we'll tackle the hard realities of this experience—learning the ropes, managing the guilt, and finding connection. And through it all, I'll remind you of the hope that comes from God's grace.

This journey isn't easy, but you don't have to walk it alone. Together, we will navigate the storm and find hope in the grace that transforms even the darkest moments. And with God, there is always hope.

Chapter One

connection

> *3 The Father of compassion and the God of comfort, 4 who comforts us in all our troubles, so that we can comfort those in any trouble with the comfort we ourselves receive from God.*
>
> 2 Corinthians 1:3–4[3]

Here we go again. The thought rattled in my mind like an unwelcome passenger as I climbed into my car, the engine humming in the icy January morning. A six-hour drive lay ahead, a route I knew too well. But this time, it wasn't just about the miles. It was about a mother's instinct, the unshakable pull in my gut that told me something wasn't right.

I hadn't heard from my son since Thanksgiving. He'd skipped Christmas and New Year's Eve without so much as a text. And when a childhood friend of his tragically died in December, he hadn't shown up for the family. That absence—so uncharacteristic—hit me like a red flag I couldn't ignore.

I was mad, upset, and a little concerned. My accountability meeting could wait; I had something far more pressing to do. So instead of sitting with my personal development group, I picked up the phone and called the Fairbanks Police to request a wellness check on my 22-year-old son.

This wasn't the first time I'd done it, but something about this call felt different. It wasn't just about finding out if he was okay. It was about something deeper: a growing determination to rebuild the fractured relationship between us.

The drive gave me too much time to think. Memories of our strained communication, of moments missed and words left unsaid, looped in my mind. Somewhere along the way, I realized the distance between us—both physical and emotional—had grown far too wide. I couldn't keep waiting for him to close the gap.

In this chapter, I'll share with you my journey, my struggles and all that led to my son's incarceration. How I've identified the theme of disconnection as a pattern that was created in my childhood, and how it wove through my entire life, marriages, children and work connections.

About an hour into the drive, my phone rang. I didn't recognize the number, but I answered anyway, heart pounding.

"Hi, Mom," came his voice, cautious and a little irritated. "Did you seriously send the cops to check on me?"

I pulled into a gas station and exhaled a breath I didn't realize I'd been holding. "It got you to call, didn't it? When can I see you? Are you going to be home tonight?"

There was hesitation in his voice, but eventually, he agreed to meet me at 4:30 p.m. As I hung up, I felt the tiniest flicker of hope—a fragile ember in the cold Alaskan winter.

Reflections on the Drive

As I continued my drive, I reflected on how we got to this place of rare communication.

All my life, I have searched for personal connection. Growing up, I struggled to find a sense of belonging, always feeling like an outsider looking in. In my marriage, there were moments of deep love, but also long stretches of disconnection. With my children, I connected through our travels together. I tried to make up for the distance by being overly lenient—a choice I feared encouraged poor choices.

But that drive on January 8, 2022, was a turning point. It marked the moment I stopped waiting for connection to come to me and started actively seeking it. It wasn't easy, and it didn't happen overnight. But step by step, I began to rebuild the relationship with my son, and in the process, I found something even greater: a connection to God that has transformed every part of my life.

Childhood Reflections:
Connection, Divorce, and Belonging

I thought about my own childhood, how patterns of disconnection seemed to repeat across generations, and how I had unknowingly carried those lessons into my own relationships.

Connection wasn't something that came naturally to me, at least not the kind that required vulnerability. Growing up in Western Massachusetts, my family seemed picture-perfect on the outside. My dad was a beloved teacher, my mom baked cookies for church bazaars, and our weekends were filled with cross-country skiing and canoeing. Yet, there was always a sense of unease, a shadow of fear I didn't understand.

When my dad said, "We need to talk," my stomach would churn with dread. What had I done wrong? Most of the time, his words weren't scolding, but the fear lingered. Looking back, I realise those moments shaped the way I approached relationships—guarded, always bracing for the other shoe to drop.

It wasn't that I didn't love my family. I adored my dad. Sitting beside him, watching the evening news, felt like a connection to me. My mom and I bonded over baking and folding endless church newsletters. But when my parents divorced, everything changed. At twelve, I didn't fully grasp what was happening. One day, we were packing to move to Vermont, the next, we were camping in a friend's field because the plan had fallen apart.

We moved to a house in the area called Rustic Ridge. Dwight L Moody had opened the Northfield School for girls in 1879. He also hosted religious conferences, which led to the development of the Rustic Ridge Association in 1901. It is a community of both seasonal cottages and year-round homes; some cottages date back 100 years. The area is very busy in the summer and quiet in the winter—our family gravitated to these semi-isolated areas.

We made memories in that house. I remember my dad building a timber-frame cabin. When the town inspectors came, they said he needed a permit. Dad's response: "I can dismantle this cabin in a day—there are no nails—and reassemble it anywhere, so it is not a permanent structure." He got a permit.

When my dad moved out to live with another woman, my confusion turned into anger—anger I directed at my mom. "He wouldn't have left if nothing was wrong," I told her cruelly. Those words still sting when I remember them.

The divorce marked the first time I truly felt disconnected. My dad remained in my life, driving me to and from school each day, but it wasn't the same. I started searching for connection elsewhere, desperate to fill the void. By thirteen, I was experimenting with alcohol, boys, and risky behavior. It wasn't a connection I was finding; it was a distraction. The shame from those years followed me into adulthood, seeping into my first marriage and every relationship that came after. I yearned so deeply to feel close to someone, but I didn't know how to open up without fear of rejection or judgment.

My First Marriage: A Journey of Love, Loss, and Lessons

We were married in Alaska, surrounded by the vast beauty of the land, but within a year, I had already broken our bond. I had been baptized in the family Baptist church, but my heart hadn't truly changed. When we sought guidance from the local pastor, the blame was placed on my husband. I think he felt obligated—as a Christian—to stay and work things out, but I wonder now if leaving early on would have saved us both years of heartache. Then again, if we had parted ways then, I wouldn't have my two children.

For five years, we struggled to hold on, trying to mend something that was fractured from the start. Eventually, we decided to have a child, as if that might anchor us. Nine months after seeing the doctor, we welcomed Takodah. I had always worked, so when my maternity leave ended, I was caught off guard by how hard it was to leave him at three months old. But once I returned to my job, I found a rhythm in balancing work and motherhood.

In May 2000, when Takodah was ten months old, we moved back to Alaska. His dad had been offered a permanent position, and I was told I would have chances too. That did not materialise because my work was seasonal, not permanent. The idea of being a stay-at-home mom had never fit me—that was my mother, my mother-in-law, but not me. Thankfully, we found a welcoming church community that helped me adjust, even moving us into our log house when my husband was away on assignment.

By 2002, our daughter was born, and my longing to work outside the home only grew stronger. In 2006, I finally stepped into a role that felt like a perfect fit—working for the Alaska Cooperative Extension Service on a fire prevention project called Firewise. For the first time, I was using my degree in a meaningful way within my own community. It felt like a turning point, but it lasted only a year.

2007 was a year that unraveled everything. My father-in-law passed away in July, and a local trial gripped our small town—a husband had shot his wife after discovering her affair. My husband was in the jury selection pool but had to withdraw. That's when I knew we had reached a point from which we could never recover. That trial forced old wounds to the surface, reminding him of my infidelity. In that moment, I realized whatever fragile thread remained between us had finally snapped.

By 2008, our marriage dissolved. I reassured myself that at least the children were young—surely, they wouldn't be as affected as I had been when my own parents divorced at thirteen. But I've since learned: there is no good age for parents to split.

Our divorce was amicable. We wrote the papers together, dividing debts, retirement, and the house without a fight. The children and I stayed in our home, while he kept his retirement.

Lessons in Hindsight

Looking back, I see the patterns—the fractures that were there from the beginning, the ways I tried to fill the voids, the ways he carried hurt that I couldn't heal. I see now that staying married without healing doesn't restore love; it deepens the wounds. Love can't be forced, and neither can redemption—it has to be chosen, lived, and grown into.

Most of all, I see that divorce, no matter how amicable, is still a breaking. No matter their age, children still feel the cracks.

New Marriage New Distance

Leaving my children with their father and stepmother in 2010 was a decision that carried both practical reasoning and deep emotional weight. The tipping points came when my children's friends asked their stepmother—who was a substitute teacher—if my kids could spend the weekend with them. I remember the surge of indignation: *How dare they ask her? I have primary custody!* Looking back, I realize how misplaced that anger was. Children's friends don't understand custody arrangements; they just see the adults in a household.

That moment made me confront the need for change. I made the difficult choice to seek a job in Anchorage, moving three and a half hours away from my children.

I believed my anger was justified, but in truth, I was grappling with a deeper loss of control over my role as their mother. When making big life decisions, it's crucial to step back and recognize the true source of our emotions before acting on them. I often told friends, "There were too many Mrs. ***'s." It was a bond that had to bend, but in hindsight, I wish I had been more focused on healing rather than running.

Patterns of my life repeated: in May 2009, I met my future husband online. As before, alcohol and promiscuity were present. But unlike before, this relationship grew into something more lasting. By August, we were already saying "I love you," and by Valentine's Day, I knew I would have proposed if he hadn't beaten me to it.

In spring 2010, a ride-along in a friend's work van introduced me to a new job opportunity. By early June, I had relocated to Anchorage, starting training just a week before my second wedding. On June 5, 2010, we married in an intimate gathering with my two children and his two girls present. Surrounded by a handful of dear friends and family. My mother officiated. Our one-night honeymoon reflected the values we shared: hard work and making the most of the little time we had together.

Our courtship may have echoed my past patterns, but our marriage began in love—real, steady, and committed. It was the kind of love that chose to endure, the kind that builds a life together even when the beginning isn't perfect.

Without Healing, History Repeats Itself

Despite experiencing the pain of broken relationships before, I still rushed into love without breaking the cycle of past wounds. I was searching for stability, but I hadn't built it within myself first. Real change only happens when we take the time to heal and grow before jumping into new commitments.

I enjoyed my new job as it combined testing, education, and driving. I always found peace in driving—a practice that has long connected me to nature. Before moving to Anchorage, when I lived in Gakona, I drove two hours with the kids to get food for our goats and chickens. At the time, it was just about the destination, but one Saturday, I told my kids, "We need to stop and enjoy the scenery, not just drive through it." That moment changed the way I viewed our journeys, making them about connection rather than just routine.

Although I had moved away, I made the most of the time I had with my children. I picked them up every other Friday, and we spent weekends hiking, canoeing, and playing board games with my husband and his two daughters. The time we spent together was intentional, and I learned that physical distance doesn't have to mean emotional distance—consistent effort and presence are what truly strengthen relationships.

There were still difficult moments, like when Takodah confided in me during a hike that he had been the last person to kiss a girl before she committed suicide. At the time, I didn't have the words to fix it, but I could offer him my presence—I hugged him and walked beside him, letting him know he wasn't alone. Years later, as I was writing this book, I learned the shocking truth: the story wasn't real. When I asked him why he had said it, his response cut deep—"I wanted to be depressed."

That revelation was both heartbreaking and eye-opening. It reminded me how much pain he had been holding in, pain I might never have uncovered had we not kept talking. Never give up on your children, no matter their age. Keep asking, keep listening, and keep creating space for truth to surface. I am so thankful for God's revelation, for the opportunity to learn about his past struggles, and for the chance to continue walking alongside him with understanding and grace.

Through the years, Takodah and I stayed connected despite my move. He worked around his school and job schedules, graduated early, and even helped me coach junior cross-country skiers—allowing me to share a lifelong passion with him. I cherished those moments, but life has a way of shifting again.

In 2019, when he and his high school girlfriend moved to Fairbanks for his job as a chef, our communication dwindled. I assumed it was just the natural busyness of life, but in reality, I could have leaned in more. If I hadn't had his girlfriend's number, I wouldn't have even known how he was doing.

It's easy to assume that our loved ones will reach out when they need us, but sometimes, they don't. Checking in, even when things seem fine, shows them they matter and helps prevent unintentional disconnection.

When I reflect on my life, I notice a pattern: disconnection, mistakes, and guilt, followed by moments of forgiveness that gradually stitch the broken pieces together. The move to Alaska with my first husband was supposed to be a fresh start, but old wounds don't heal just because you change your surroundings. We both brought our fears—my shame and his broken trust—and they chipped away at our marriage until there was nothing left.

By the time I remarried, I thought I had figured it out, but I still carried unresolved struggles. I have an incredibly supportive husband now, and know that with continuous prayer, any disconnection will be repaired.

***

As I pulled back onto the road, the weight of our strained relationship seemed to settle into the passenger seat beside me. I didn't know what awaited me at the end of the drive, but one thing was clear: I couldn't let fear or pride hold me back anymore.

Sometimes, healing begins with nothing more than a mother's stubborn hope and the courage to drive forward, no matter how uncertain the road ahead.

This chapter lays the foundation for the journey that was to unfold. You, too, will have your own journey, your own challenges, and your own story that led to the unfolding of the unthinkable.

As I think about "the unthinkable," I feel the quiet pull of something larger than myself. That sense of guidance, of being watched over, it was there even before I fully understood it. Every year on January 8—the date I reconnected with my son—I say a silent prayer. In 2022, I didn't have a relationship with God, but I always knew there was something bigger than me controlling everything. Today, I am so grateful to have found my ultimate connection: God. It is this desire for meaningful connection that drives me to help other mothers, fathers, friends, and family to connect with their incarcerated loved ones.

In the next chapter, you'll discover how I navigated the discovery of my son's incarceration—and how you can too.

Chapter Two

SHOCK

The Lord is close to the brokenhearted and saves those who are crushed in spirit.

Psalm 34:18 [4]

Wednesday, January 19, 2022, started like any other January day in Alaska. The days were short, but Valentine's Day wasn't far away—a marker I always told newcomers to aim for. "If you can just make it to Valentine's Day," I'd say, "you'll feel the day length change. You can say you've survived winter."

I am an early riser, and it was 24°F at 6 a.m.—almost balmy by Alaskan standards, especially compared to Fairbanks's 2°F. Ah, I thought, another beautiful morning in Alaska. Coffee cup in hand, I headed down the stairs, put on my shoes, went through the garage, and stepped outside. The cold bit at my cheeks, but it was the kind of cold you could work with. It made me feel tough. Capable. Ready.

Then I entered my studio office tucked among the birch trees, just seven steps from the garage. Thankfully, it felt cozy and warm from the in-floor heating my husband had lovingly installed years ago. My mom, who had visited me wherever I'd lived since my first marriage, moved to Alaska in 2015 with the plan of living in the studio. While it was being finished, she stayed in our basement bedroom. Then life had other plans. She found love and ended up moving in with him, leaving me with the studio ready to make my own.

I sat down, opened Facebook, and started to scroll, as was my habit. I was not at all prepared for what I read.

Staring back at me was a mugshot of my son! A total stranger had put a comment on my post: *Takodah is a person of interest in a murder investigation.*

My first thought: I have to get this post off my Facebook before my mom—his grandmother—sees this. What will she think? I didn't even know what to think.

Shock.

That's truly what it was—that first moment, that whole day. It was a tidal wave of disbelief.

The comment had been posted on an old picture I'd shared years ago—Takodah and me at the Fairbanks airport. I had flown up to celebrate his birthday with him and his girlfriend, and that snapshot was taken as I was leaving. He looked happy, radiant even. We biked, canoed, and enjoyed Fourth of July festivities in the quaint little town of Ester. I remember feeling so grateful, so thrilled that we'd celebrated both his birthday and this holiday together. It was a memory I had cherished. Until it became the place where the unthinkable landed: a stranger linking my son's name to a murder and the Fairbanks Police Department.

I deleted the comment immediately. Not just to protect myself—but my mom. She checks Facebook. What if she saw the notification? What if this photo, this memory, was the way she found out?

I didn't want to believe it. I couldn't. I had just been to Fairbanks ten days earlier. I had finally reached a point where our communication, or lack of it, was weighing too heavily on me. I was tired of the silence—calling, texting, leaving voicemails with no reply. So I drove 365 miles just to see him in person.

We met that Saturday. He couldn't go out to dinner, but we agreed to have breakfast the next morning. We said 7:00. He showed up at 7:30—with his new girlfriend. Still, we sat and talked. We made a plan: we'd talk every Thursday. And we did. The following Thursday, we had a good call. I had such high hopes.

Now here I was—seeing his name connected to something horrifying, and with no idea what to believe.

I picked up my phone and called him. I wasn't expecting him to answer, but I had to try. It went to voicemail. I left a message, my voice shaking.

"Takodah, I saw a stranger post about you being a person of interest. If you had an accident and hit someone, go to the police. You have to let them know what happened."

I waited. Fifteen minutes. An hour. All day. I kept hoping he'd call me back and say everything was okay—that he had already turned himself in, or better yet, that this was some big mistake. But the silence from him lasted all day long.

Enter the first stage of grief—denial, numbness, shock. I had just spoken to my son on Thursday. I went right into excuse mode for him. There has to be some reasonable explanation. Have you ever done this for your child? It truly is a common reaction when grief comes at us with little warning. It has taken growing my relationship with God and my son to stop making excuses for him. It took me a good two years, so please don't beat yourself up if you are still at that stage. And it can be just a stage.

Being a mom, I wanted to know what was going on. Facebook will show you more than you ever need to know. I quickly went to the police department's Facebook page, and the comments started flooding in. Some were supportive, some confused, and others cruel:

"I'm baffled right now... what went down!? This guy helped Girl Scouts set up garden harvesting for a soup kitchen like... four years ago, maybe... I'm so lost."

"Didn't you go out with him?"

I read more and more. One comment mentioned seeing him at a restaurant the night before with a girl. I knew the restaurant. That made it feel even more real—and even more baffling.

It was 8:00 a.m., and the house was empty. I had to get ready for work—leading my students at the Senior Center in exercise classes over

Zoom. My husband and stepdaughter were already at work, and my youngest stepdaughter was at school. I wanted nothing more than to stay home, but people were counting on me, so at 8:15, I left.

I don't really remember the drive. My mind kept repeating: *this can't be real, there must be a mistake.* The most disturbing question was, why would he be around people who made him that angry?

I got through my two classes and then headed to my newest Airbnb studio apartment at 10:45 a.m. While waiting for the internet technician, I checked my messages for what felt like the tenth time, then opened Facebook. The comments continued to be a mix of shock and negative remarks. I texted a close friend I'd met through my personal development classes to let her know the studio now had internet. Then I drove home. Still numb. Still in disbelief. Could this actually be real?

When I got back, I went straight to my studio office. I needed to let someone else know that my world had just been turned upside down. Only yesterday, I'd been talking with my friend about how life can change in "a heartbeat." And here was proof.

Now, sending her a Facebook message, she was exactly what I needed. She didn't try to fix it. She just listened. And that was enough. Sometimes, all you need is one person in your corner.

Looking back, I realize how fragile I felt in those first days. I was angry, scared, and numb all at once—overwhelmed as if the ground had shifted under my feet. At that time, I didn't have a close relationship with God. I felt lost. But even then, something bigger was quietly holding me together—carrying me when I didn't even recognize it.

If you find yourself in that place too, I want you to know it's okay to feel what you feel. You don't have to be strong every second. It's enough to breathe, to take the next small step, to find one safe person who will simply listen. You are not alone, even if it feels like the world has turned its back.

In the middle of the storm, peace can feel impossible. But I believe even the smallest spark of peace is there, waiting for you.

I didn't have any answers and needed to shovel a driveway of the house I managed, so we didn't message back and forth long. I was thankful it gave me something physical to do—something normal.

Around 3:00 p.m., my phone rang, just as I was pulling up to the house needing shoveling. It was my 19-year-old daughter. She never calls during the week. My heart dropped.

She knows.

I answered with forced calm, "Hi honey, how are you?"

She asked, gently but clearly, "What's going on with Takodah?"

I told her the truth, or at least what I knew. "All I know is that he's a person of interest. I left him a voicemail telling him that if it was an accident and someone died, then it's a homicide, and he needs to turn himself in."

Then I asked, "How did you find out?"

She said her ex-stepmother had called her out of concern.

Of course. The same woman I had moved three and a half hours away from to get space and peace—here she was again, inserting herself into our family's pain. Not reaching out to me, but to my daughter, who was trying to focus on school in Montana.

I could feel the anger boil. Why is she always first in line to deliver the bad news?

I told my daughter I would keep her updated, then hung up.

Now I knew—if my daughter knew, her dad probably knew. So I texted my ex-husband.

"Why is your ex-wife telling our daughter about Takodah?"

He replied, "What is up with Takodah?"

Wonderful. Now I had to tell him what little I knew.

Navigating this new reality as a mom was hard enough, but add an ex-husband into the mix, and things get even more complicated. Would he blame me? Blame himself? Thanks to personal development, I knew I couldn't take on that weight. I had learned how my childhood shaped my self-doubt and fear of confrontation, and how I tended to carry all the blame for everything that went wrong.

Just ten days before, during that drive to see Takodah, I had listened to *The Four Agreements* by Don Miguel Ruiz. That book changed me. It helped me realize how many beliefs I had accepted as truth—especially the idea that I was a bad mom. On that drive home, I finally said no to that agreement. I had always done the best I could. I loved my children. Maybe I hadn't put all the boundaries in place, but his choices were his own.

Still, I knew I needed to call his dad. Deep breath. Tap "Kids' Dad" on my contacts.

"Hi. So, I saw a post about Takodah being a person of interest with the Fairbanks Police."

His response: "What do you know? Where is he?"

"I don't know," I said. "I've tried calling. I left a message. Maybe it was an accident and somebody died."

He said, "I just spoke to him on Sunday. He talked about wanting to get out of Fairbanks, move to Colorado. There was no indication anything was wrong."

I hung up and went back to shoveling. One scoop of snow at a time—like somehow I could push the weight of this situation away with each motion. I was still numb. My mind raced. As I shoveled, slowly but steadily, I recalled my mentor's words: "How do you eat an elephant? One bite at a time." Looking back, it was truly a blessing that I had a physical task to accomplish, something that let my body move while my mind wandered.

That night, I drove home, walked out to the cabin behind the house, grabbed my laptop, and showed my husband the Fairbanks Police Facebook post. I simply stated, "This is what I've been dealing with all day." As he read, I also explained that my daughter's ex-stepmom had told her what was going on.

As unhappy as I was about that, I still said, "Can we not tell the girls?"—his daughters.

He looked at me, "Do you want them to find out like your daughter did?"

He was right, of course. So we told them. As they read the post, we explained that we really didn't know anything more. By now, the police had updated the post—not only was he a person of interest, but they had found his car. He was officially on the run.

That night, I had to make one more call—my mom. She needed to know.

"Can we come over tomorrow morning?" I asked.

"Sure," she said, unsuspecting.

"Okay. We'll see you at 9:00."

The next morning, as she opened the door, I kept my eyes on my shoes. I couldn't let her see my face. We walked up the stairs—me, my husband, my mom, and her partner. I sat on the couch next to her, rigid.

"I saw a post yesterday... about Takodah. He's a person of interest. They found his car. I've tried to call him. No answer. I even called his old girlfriend—she hasn't heard from him since November."

She didn't panic. She didn't ask a thousand questions. She just let me speak. Looking back, she was a rock. Her calm held me steady. There wasn't a lot of information to share, and we didn't stay long. Hugs were given all around.

We left knowing we were loved and supported.

And then came Saturday, January 22, 2022.

Have you ever said, Thank God my child has been arrested?

Because I did.

I was sitting in my car, parked in front of someone's house, about to look at a queen mattress on Facebook Marketplace for one of my Airbnb units. It felt like the most normal, practical thing in the world—check out the mattress, maybe haggle the price a little, load it up and keep the business going.

My phone pinged with a Facebook Messenger notification. It was Susan, my friend, whom I had reached out to on Wednesday.

"Evening, Heidi. I just went searching to see if there was any news. I just saw that 'Takodah has been apprehended by law enforcement.'"

I just stared at it for a second.

My reply was honest but flat:

"Oh geez. But good."

Because it was good. Good in the worst way possible. Good that he was alive. Good that I wasn't going to get a call from the coroner instead.

She asked if I already knew. I didn't.

"You informed me."

I could feel her horror from the other side of the screen.

"Wow. I'm kind of appalled. I'm glad you are aware."

She sent me the link. It was an update to the police department's previous post. "Person of interest" now changed to "apprehended."

I read it. I let out a breath I didn't even know I'd been holding.

I typed back:

"Our whole family thanks you."

Because we did. Because, as humiliating as it was to find out from Facebook Messenger, at least it was an answer.

Later, I would think about how weird it was to be sitting in my car, worrying about a mattress deal, when my whole world was tilting sideways. How it felt to realize that "arrested" was the best outcome I could hope for.

It's a strange kind of gratitude—to thank God your child is behind bars. But I did. I really did. Because being behind bars meant being alive.

Chapter Three

What You Need to Know Once in Jail

6 Nevertheless, the one who receives instruction in the word should share all good things with their instructor. 9 Let us not become weary in doing good, for at the proper time we will reap a harvest if we do not give up. 10 Therefore, as we have opportunity, let us do good to all people, especially to those who belong to the family of believers.

Galatians 6:6, 9–10 [5]

The moment you learn your child, sibling, partner, or friend is in jail, your world changes. The shock doesn't just end when you know where they are. Instead, it transforms into new fears: What happens now? How do you help them? How do you even talk to them?

Nothing prepares you for that moment.

I remember sitting in my car after finding out Takodah had been arrested. Relief hit me like a wave—he was alive, he was safe. But then came the next question: Now what?

That question haunted me in the quiet hours. I didn't have a handbook. I didn't have anyone to guide me on what steps to take, what rules to follow, or what mistakes to avoid. I just knew I was his mother. I needed to show up, somehow. Even when I was scared. Even when I felt completely lost.

If you're here reading this, you might be standing in that same place of confusion and fear. You might be asking: How do I stay connected? How do I help them navigate the system? What do I need to know to survive this?

I don't have all the answers. But I can tell you what I learned the hard way. Because even in the hardest season—even when you're hurt, angry, grieving, or afraid—you can still find ways to stay connected. You can learn the system. You can help them, and help yourself.

Let's talk about how.

Finding Information: DOC Websites and VINE

There's so much to learn when a loved one is incarcerated—and you often have to learn it overnight. The process can feel overwhelming, but the right resources make it easier.

Each state has its own Department of Corrections (DOC) website. It's not perfect, but it's essential. For Alaska, it lists how to locate an inmate, mail rules, phone access, visitation policies, medical services, prisoner accounts, and faith-based programs. Wherever you are, find your state's DOC site. It will become your go-to resource.

If authorities haven't contacted you—or if your loved one is being transferred—one of the first challenges is simply locating them.

The VINE (Victim Information and Notification Everyday) website (https://vinelink.com)[6] allows you to search inmates with just the first two letters of their first and last names. It's available 24/7, and you can also call 1-800-247-9763.

What you need to know is that inmates can be moved without warning, and checking periodically can ease the worry when communication suddenly stops.

Another Key Tool: CourtView

In Alaska, another resource I quickly learned to depend on was CourtView. Not every state has it, but here it's a public access website that lets you follow a case from the very first charges until it's closed after sentencing.

I can't remember exactly how I found it—maybe through a Facebook connection who reached out when she learned Takodah was a person of interest in Fairbanks. But it quickly became one of the most important tools I had.

When you first go to CourtView, you click *Search Cases*. It defaults to requesting a case number, but I didn't have that. Instead, I searched by name.

You can narrow by case status—"open" or "closed." For us, Takodah's case stayed open from January 2022 until March 2025.

Once you locate your loved one, double-check the birthday to be sure it's the right person. Then you'll see tabs with information such as:

Party: "State of Alaska vs. [your loved one]."
Charges: this can change over time.
Events: hearings, arraignments, bail hearings, trials.
Docket: all filed paperwork, from warrants to requests for counsel.

From the beginning, I checked CourtView several times a day. That's how I learned when a public defender had been assigned, and also when a conflict of interest meant we had to wait for another lawyer.

One late night in March 2022, I saw a docket entry that shook me. At 9:16 p.m., it showed Takodah had another arraignment scheduled—a court hearing where the charges are read out loud. He had already been arraigned once, right after his arrest. Why another? Just fifteen minutes later, he called, unaware of it himself. I told him, and we both felt that punch of confusion.

By the next morning, a new charge had appeared: *Murder in the First Degree (with intent to cause death)*. Reading that in black and white was crushing. CourtView gave me information in almost real-time, but it also forced me to process information I didn't always understand, sometimes before my son even knew.

If your state has a system like CourtView, I encourage you to use it. It's not always easy, but it keeps you informed, and it helps you advocate for your loved one. Just know that while information empowers you, it can also overwhelm you. Lean on others who've walked this road—they can help you make sense of what really matters.

Mail: Finding and Staying Connected with Your Loved One

If you're my age or older—Gen X but feeling more like a Baby Boomer—you might remember writing thank-you letters to grandparents, aunts, or uncles after birthdays. I remember checking the mailbox every day at summer camp, waiting for a letter from home.

That feeling of anticipation came rushing back when my son went to jail.

Mail became more than a way to communicate. It was a lifeline. A way to remind him—and myself—that he wasn't alone. Even when he was in the same town, I wrote to him often.

But jail mail has rules.

- Return address must include your full address and at least your first initial and last name.

- Only white envelopes—no cute red Valentine ones.

- You can draw on envelopes, but only with black or blue ink or graphite pencil.

- Only store-bought cards. No homemade, no 3D pop-ups, no glitter.

- No loose stamps or stickers.

- Photos must come from approved vendors like Shutterfly, Walmart, or FreePrints. Usually ten per day and twenty-five per week, but it varies.

- No provocative images.

Even little things, like sending a photo of my Easter candy bar as if Takodah had given it to me, helped us maintain a bond. He now has scrapbooks labeled "people," "scenery," "food," and "other"—the Easter candy being "other."

The key lesson? Flexibility and patience reduce frustration. Rules can change, so always check the facility's guidelines before sending anything.

Phone Communication Details

Securus is the main phone service in many facilities. It's not perfect. You can set up billing on the Securus website https://securustech.net/ [7] or by calling 1-800-844-6591.

Calls are usually limited to fifteen minutes. And remember: *they are always recorded.*

My best advice for those early calls? Keep it simple. Remind them: *This call is recorded and can be used in court.*

Ask safe, caring questions. *How are you? What did you have for lunch?*

The Power of Phone Calls

Once I found out Takodah was in jail—a pre-sentencing facility—my stomach twisted. My fingers hovered over my phone before I forced myself to call his dad, sister, and grandmother.

I remember that first call to his dad. *What can we do?*

We couldn't believe we were here. We read on the Fairbanks Police Department Facebook page about the bullet holes police found in the bathroom of the crime scene. "Takodah wouldn't use a firearm like that," his dad said, and I agreed wholeheartedly.

His dad had already contacted a defense lawyer to make enquiries. It was very expensive, he told me—especially for a murder case. The words hung between us, thick and suffocating. How did it come to this?

Within twenty-four hours of being arrested, Takodah called me. I felt privileged to get the first call.

"Mom," he said, his voice edged with urgency. "I wasn't there. My buddy woke me up when he saw the police were looking for me."

I gripped the phone tighter. "OK." I let the word hang, hoping he'd say more. Hoping he'd say something that made sense. But that was it.

I wanted to believe him. I *did* believe him. I always had—and he knew it. No matter what he told me, I never questioned him the way I could have... should have.

Maybe because I couldn't imagine him physically hurting anyone. Maybe because a mother's love has a way of blinding you to the cracks forming right in front of you.

I wanted to ask, *Why didn't you turn yourself in?* But I swallowed it. The automated Securus message had warned me: *This is not a private call.*

I didn't know who was listening. I didn't want to back him into a corner.

Deep down, I wanted to keep hope alive—that maybe, just maybe, he was telling the truth.

Major Lesson Learned About Lawyers

Your loved one might be arraigned within hours or a day or two. In our case, it was Sunday morning; four days after the initial missing person announcement. If they refuse a public defender, they'll have to complete paperwork later to request one—and that can take time.

It's easy to feel frustrated or helpless. But knowing the process helps you advocate without adding confusion.

One of the hardest, earliest lessons: *Tell your loved one to accept the public defender (PD)—even if you're thinking about hiring a lawyer.*

It took us three weeks to get a PD assigned.

Takodah went to his first arraignment on Sunday—the day after his arrest. He refused the PD then, thinking we'd hire one privately. But once it became clear we couldn't afford it, he had to file paperwork to request one.

Three weeks passed as they sorted through conflicts of interest. My assumption as to why there were so many? The local PDs had represented the deceased or injured victims in the past.

Eventually, after twenty-eight long days, the courts assigned a contracted firm. We learned that PD offices are overloaded with cases, and hiring a contracted firm meant they were only paid for time spent consulting with our son, not us, his concerned parents.

Don't expect much communication with the PD. From the start, we were informed that Takodah was *their* client—not us. They advised him not to waive the attorney-client privilege, which meant we, as his parents, had no right to information or input on his legal decisions. It can feel frustrating, but I believe this was necessary to maintain the integrity of his case.

Visitation: Navigating the System

Visitation rules vary by facility, but there are common themes:

- **ID:** Bring a valid photo ID. Temporary paper IDs often aren't accepted.

- **Minors:** Must have a birth certificate and an adult with them.

- **Dress code:** Modest clothing. No hoodies, ripped jeans, leggings, or revealing outfits.

- **No personal belongings:** Leave phones, keys, and extras in the car or a locker.

- **Sign-up:** Some facilities require the inmate to request visits; others need you to call ahead or arrive early.

Even locker systems vary. Some need a quarter. Some hold your ID for a key. Some have open cubbies with no security.

At first, these rules felt overwhelming. I kept a spare set of clothes in my car in case I was denied entry. Over time, I developed a routine: jeans, plain shirt, and always planning for a locker.

It got easier. Not easy—but easier.

Closing Reflection

I didn't want to learn any of this. I didn't want to become an expert in jail mail rules, visitation policies, or Securus billing.

But love demands it.

When someone you care about is incarcerated, you don't just grieve what happened—you grieve the future you thought you'd have. The future you thought *they* might have. You wrestle with blame, guilt, anger, and fear. And in the middle of it all, you have to learn how to *stay connected*.

It's messy. It's emotional. But it's also essential.

If you're reading this and feeling overwhelmed, that's totally okay. I was. There's no perfect way to do this. No way to make it painless. But there are ways to make it possible.

Give yourself grace. Give them grace, too—even if you don't know yet what the future holds.

Connection doesn't fix everything. But it keeps the door open for healing.

And that is something worth fighting for.

Chapter Four

A New Jail, A New Reality

11 I am not saying this because I am in need, for I have learned to be content whatever the circumstances. 12 I know what it is to be in need, and I know what it is to have plenty. I have learned the secret of being content in any and every situation, whether well fed or hungry, whether living in plenty or in want. 13 I can do all this through him who gives me strength.

Philippians 4:11–13 [8]

April 2022. My phone rings.

That number doesn't look familiar. But if you're like me, by now you've probably started answering every random number that comes through. Toll-free, out-of-state, local numbers you've never seen—it doesn't matter. When your child is incarcerated, every ring might be the one that finally connects you to them.

I slide my finger across the screen and lift the phone to my ear. That now-familiar Securus voice clicks on:

"You have a prepaid call from... Takodah... an inmate at Anchorage Correctional Complex. You may begin the call."

Wait—Anchorage? I thought he was in Fairbanks.

I'm momentarily disoriented. Did I hear that right?

"Hi, Takodah," I say, startled but steady. "You're in Anchorage?"

"Hi, Mom," he says.

And just like that, my heart softens. No matter what has happened, no matter where he is, I can always hear his sweetness in those two words: "Hi, Mom." His voice carries so much—his love, his longing, his regret. I can almost feel the boy in him soften on the other end of the line.

"Yeah, they told me about 11 p.m. to pack up my stuff," he says. "One big box allowed. They said don't bring any clothes—they don't allow sweatpants or T-shirts in Anchorage."

So sudden. So procedural. Like it was just another item on someone's to-do list.

He tells me about his ride down in a transport van. They stopped halfway to exchange inmates and eat a bologna sandwich—nothing fancy, just the standard weekend fare. He chuckles a little, describing it, and I imagine him holding that sandwich, maybe half-laughing at the absurdity of it all.

But then his tone softens. "Mom," he says, "I got to see the mountains."

He did have a window in Fairbanks to see the sky, but the mountains—that was a special treat. I could hear his appreciation and longing tucked into those five words.

It had been a long two months of being locked inside gray walls, seeing nothing but concrete and steel, staring at the same dull ceiling day after day. And now, out the window of a moving van, for a few hours on the highway, the world opened up.

He described the mountains to me the way someone describes a dream they're afraid to forget—white peaks against the winter sky, shadows dancing across ridgelines, the light sharp and real. Even through the glass, even in chains, they gave him something. A breath. A reminder that beauty still existed, even if it was just passing by.

He's always been that way—drawn to nature. I called him my mountain goat—if it could be climbed, there he would be. The mountains were never just background for him. They were steady, grounding. A form of prayer before either of us even had a word for it.

He also mentioned how good it felt just to talk to other people again. After two months of near-total isolation, even brief conversations with other inmates during the transfer felt oddly normal. But it was the mountains that really struck him—like a breath of fresh air after holding it in too long.

Now he's in booking at Anchorage—the intake area where new arrivals are processed—still waiting to find out which unit (or "mod," as the jail calls them) he'll be placed in. There's that low hum of uncertainty—new guards, new inmates, new rhythm. But the way he spoke about that view of the mountains... I could hear something in him I hadn't heard in a long time.

Not happiness exactly. But light. Memory. Something alive.

A moment of light doesn't change everything, but it reminds you that change is still possible.

To the parent reading this—hold onto those glimpses of light. They won't look like what you expect. Sometimes it's the softness in your child's voice. Sometimes it's a moment when they describe something beautiful they saw, even if only for a second. These moments remind us that the person we love is still in there, still feeling, still hoping.

God was there that day, even though I didn't recognize it at the time. I see now that He gave Takodah a glimpse of His creation to whisper, "You're not forgotten." If your child has ever shared something small but meaningful—a song, a memory, a view—treasure it. That's God, showing up in the middle of concrete and chains.

That phone call was a small crack of light in a very dark time. Just hearing Takodah's voice, and especially his words about the mountains, reminded me that no matter how harsh the walls or how heavy the chains, the world outside—and the hope inside—still existed.

The phone call ended, but the journey didn't. That call became the first step into a new rhythm, one that came with new logistics, new routines—and new courage.

Having resources helped when Takodah was transported from Fairbanks to Anchorage in April, just two months after his arrest. I searched the

DOC (Department of Corrections) pages, looked up the facility, and figured out the process. Once I was told he was on the West side (many facilities have multiple buildings), I could call and set up a visit. This was so different from Fairbanks, where Takodah had to arrange the visit and put us on the list. Here, all I had to do was call and say, "I'd like to visit on Tuesday at 7:00 p.m."

Each change in this journey was nerve-racking, and it jarred me every time. The usual thoughts run through your mind: *Am I going to be approved? How long does it take? Did I fill out the form correctly?* You'd think having a degree would make me confident, but it feels new every time. I've come to realize I need to give myself grace and trust that God knows my fears—He listens every day.

You may get a gruff front desk person, but they are there to answer your questions. Remember, they work in a jail, dealing with unhappy, stressed people every day.

I was thrilled. Now that he was in Anchorage, my family and I could see Takodah more easily. I didn't think too deeply about why he was transferred—maybe for safety from the gang members, I supposed—but I wouldn't allow myself to dwell on that thought. I still didn't fully grasp the danger my son could experience in jail. He was in Administrative Solitary confinement when initially arrested because of the charges.

Moving to Anchorage, he was in Protective Custody, which came with more freedoms, like going outside and being without handcuffs. Now, looking back, I see how God protected him every step of the way. It is through witnessing God's grace in all of this that we have both come to know Him deeply. We can see and feel that we are protected and blessed.

I had no experience and no one to ask. I wanted to believe, to say that everything would be all right—but would it? At least now, I knew where to go to learn how visiting worked.

The First Visit: Stepping Into the Unknown

I remember being so nervous on the first visit. I have to admit—I have a demanding spirit. I told my mom and the rest of the family that I wanted to visit Takodah by myself. Maybe I wanted to be the first to see him in his new place. Or maybe I thought we could be more raw with each other without anyone else around. Either way, I got my wish. That April, I visited him alone.

The waiting room was nothing like Fairbanks. There were three walls lined with chairs, a half-wall of lockers, a barely maintained bathroom, a receptionist's desk, and a door leading to the correctional officers' break room. There was no metal detector like in Fairbanks. Slowly, other women entered and took seats. A few shy smiles were exchanged, but no one spoke. It was 6:00 p.m. Check-in started at 6:15.

As I sat waiting, my mind raced. *I don't want to be first. I don't want to stand out. How will he look after a month in jail?*

By 6:10, the small waiting room had filled up. Women stood and formed a line, so I followed, taking my place at the end. It was April—no longer cold—but I had brought my purse and car keys. I had called ahead and asked, "Where do I put my purse?" They told me there were lockers for a quarter. So I had my quarter ready.

One by one, we checked in at the receptionist's desk.

"Inmate's last name?"

"First name?"

"ID, please."

They marked our names in the same box as our loved ones on a sheet, checked the computer, and confirmed the cell and bunk numbers.

Now, we waited.

Did I mention? No cell phone usage in the visitor's room. No mindlessly scrolling to get through the next forty-five minutes. Just waiting. Eventually, I learned to use that time to read and prepare to talk to Takodah—not just about daily life, but about my Bible study.

At exactly 7:00 p.m., the room grew restless. People shifted in their seats, eyes darting to the window.

Through the glass, I could see an elevator door, a large round corner mirror—the kind you'd find on a sharp turn in the road to help you see oncoming cars—and two doors, one to the left and one to the right.

This was it.

Locked In Together

The head correctional officer, the CO, entered the waiting room, holding the door open. Everyone instinctively moved to the side, making way for him.

When it was my turn, I followed the protocol. I held out my hands and spread my feet while the officer used a metal detector wand—first on my front, then my back, even checking the bottoms of my feet. Once cleared, I was directed toward a door on the right. Most people went to the elevator, but I was pointed in a different direction.

Another mom had already gone in before me. When I stepped inside, I saw her sitting in a small room. I pushed open the next door, entering the visitation area. It was a tiny cubicle, no more than four feet by six. A plastic chair sat in front of a desk with a large, thick window separating visitors from inmates. A telephone was mounted on the left side.

As I sat and waited, I saw a guard walking beside my son. He was dressed in orange—something I had quickly learned carried meaning in jail.

During one of our visits, a group of five inmates walked by, all dressed in white. Curious, I asked Takodah what the different colors meant. He explained: *white* was for the kitchen crew, *orange* was segregation, and *yellow* was general population. *Red*—he didn't go into detail, but I understood enough to know it meant something serious.

His hands were cuffed behind his back as they moved through the hall. From the left, the officer led him to the door, uncuffed him, and Takodah stepped inside.

He sat down, and the moment both doors clicked shut behind him, the sound echoed through the small room—a sharp, final reminder that we were locked in. The weight of it settled over me like a heavy fog. There was no mistaking it now. He was on one side of the glass, and I was on the other. Two different worlds, divided by inches but separated by so much more.

Routine and Realities of Jail Life

After that, my mom and I settled into a routine. We visited together every Monday, Wednesday, and Friday. The correctional officers were kind enough to put two chairs in the tiny 4x6 room, though the desk still took up half the space. The phone cords were short, making conversations awkward, but we made it work.

Over the next six months, I settled into a routine. The phone reception was unreliable, sometimes cutting out mid-conversation. Some visitors, particularly the women who went upstairs, often complained that their phones didn't work at all. I started recognizing familiar faces, including another mother who, like me, was a regular visitor in the cubicles to the right.

Takodah told me about the other inmates, sharing names and stories of their interactions. His unit was small—five cells on the first floor, five on the second. Each inmate had their own space. A shared television sat in a spot where everyone could see it.

One day, Takodah told me a funny story about the TV. He had been watching for months, not realizing that a certain radio station played the corresponding audio. He had headphones and a radio but never knew to tune in. So, for half a year, he had been watching programs with no sound, only realizing later that he could have been listening the whole time.

It reminded me that we weren't the only ones learning—those on the inside had to adjust, too. Everything was new, unfamiliar, and confusing, especially for those experiencing the system for the first time.

Finding Community

One day, in the waiting room, I noticed another mother I had seen before. I finally got the courage to approach her.

"I'm Heidi," I said. "Takodah's mom."

She smiled invitingly, with a touch of knowing.

"My son is in the same mod," she replied.

And just like that, a friendship began.

Chapter Five
Our Faith Walk

5 Those who live according to the flesh have their minds set on what the flesh desires; but those who live in accordance with the Spirit have their minds set on what the Spirit desires.

Romans 8:5 [9]

I remember growing up and seeing *Our Daily Bread* devotionals around. They were appealing because of the application stories, though I never really paid attention to the full content—just the verses.

One day, during a visit, Takodah asked me, "Do you read the chapter and verses that are bolded at the top?" (underlined in blue in the picture below)

"No," I said. "I didn't even realize there was more to read."

That moment was humbling—and funny. It reminded me that sometimes our children teach us what we overlook.

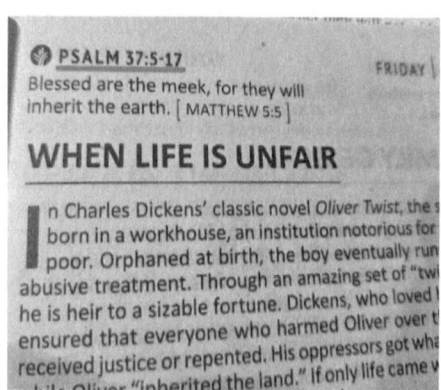

We began reading *Our Daily Bread* together regularly during visits. It gave us a shared topic—so helpful when you're worried that your conversations might not feel relevant to their world inside. But I learned that Takodah loved hearing that I was still out hiking and doing the things we used to love. You have to know your child—some need distance, others need inclusion. For Takodah, it helped him feel connected.

Sitting across from Takodah while he asked me about the chapter and verses bolded at the top of *Our Daily Bread* reminded me how much I'd been skimming—through devotionals and maybe even through life. He was paying attention. He was hungry for more. And now I was too.

Bible Study by Mail

At Anchorage Correctional Complex, chaplains regularly visited the different mods. One day, Takodah learned he could request Bible studies by filling out a form. He sent me a copy of his Bible study on the book of Matthew, and it became our first official Bible study together.

That reignited something in me.

The flame to know God—to really understand the Bible—came back. I realized the personal development journey I'd been on, especially through Darren Hardy's influence, had parallels with scripture. Many of the principles Darren taught were actually rooted in biblical wisdom.

I had been involved in personal development and direct sales businesses that felt very pushy about following God. I didn't connect with that part, so I just let it slide—I let them talk and I just waited for the next lesson. But through doing Bible studies with Takodah, I saw all the connections. And I was blown away. There they were, all this time.

I'd been around faith before, but this time it wasn't about pressure. This was personal. This was real.

Then Takodah started doing Bible studies through EmmausWorldwide.org.[10] He told me about it, and I looked it up on Google. I found the same studies and started doing them too. Now we had something in common to discuss during every visit. It gave us a rhythm—something spiritual, intellectual, and emotional we could share. We weren't just passing time; we were growing.

He also received the first book in the Tim LaHaye *Left Behind* series, which describes the Rapture—where some passengers on a Boeing 747 just disappear while others are left behind. Reading those books alongside Takodah was so fulfilling. We'd agree on how many chapters to tackle each night and then talk through what we had read. We even stumbled over pronouncing some of the names, but it was exciting to explore the story together—wondering aloud, *Would we be left behind? Or would we be snatched up immediately?*

Even today, I remember those conversations as an invitation to examine my own life: *Am I surrendering myself fully to Christ, or am I being superficial and just going through the motions?*

There was something sacred about reading the same words at the same time, even from miles apart. The Bible studies through Emmaus gave us a shared anchor, while the *Left Behind* series challenged our imaginations and our beliefs. What started as a tool to fill the silence between us became a lifeline—both to each other and to God.

Rediscovering Church

As we got deeper into our routines, I felt a longing to return to church.

When Takodah's younger sister was born, my then-husband, Takodah, and I were staying in a friend's apartment in Anchorage while waiting for her birth. During that time, we attended a nearby church—a big red one. It was warm and inviting, the kind of place that left an impression. So when I felt that pull toward church again, my heart went back to that place.

But twenty years had passed, and when I returned, it wasn't the same.

The main sanctuary was closed—likely due to COVID—and services were now held in a smaller annex. The congregation was Samoan, and while the service was beautiful and rich with tradition, it didn't resonate with me personally. I stayed for the service, but I knew I hadn't found my place yet.

So I walked—literally—through the woods to another church: Anchorage Baptist Temple.

This church was huge and, frankly, a bit intimidating on the outside. But from the moment I stepped in, I was welcomed—by greeters at the door, by ushers in the sanctuary. And then the praise music started. Every song was drenched in worship. My heart softened, and without realizing it, I had found my home.

God's providence is stunning. The faith-based mod that Takodah would later be accepted into was connected to this very church. The relationships I built there have guided both my son and me. I cannot emphasize this enough—find a church home. I pray you experience one as welcoming as ours.

> *"Let us not give up meeting together, as some are in the habit of doing, but encouraging one another—and all the more as you see the Day approaching." (Hebrews 10:25)*[11]

Returning to church wasn't just about religion—it was about belonging. About connection. About finding a space where both my healing and Takodah's could take root and grow. I didn't expect God to connect our journeys through the same church building, but He did. When you're searching for hope, don't be afraid to walk through unfamiliar doors. God might already be waiting inside.

Year of Prayers

Takodah's public defender had suggested we request a bail hearing to determine whether he could be released from custody, while awaiting trial. At this stage, Takodah had been charged but not yet tried or sentenced.

Bail comes with many conditions, and we needed a plan. We knew he would need 24-hour surveillance. He couldn't be left alone, and he'd have to wear an ankle monitor so the parole officer always knew where he was. My mom, husband, and I had brainstormed how we could manage supervision while I worked.

My mom agreed to come to our home while I was away. She knew how impactful my teaching was, so she wanted to help out as much as possible. We set up a schedule, even allowed time for me to attend some of the races my husband would compete in all summer at the local racetrack.

Once we had a plan, the first hearing was scheduled for May 2022.

We were hoping the court might reduce the exorbitant bail amount to something our family could manage, so that Takodah could be home with us until his trial date.

Together, my mom, ex-husband and I, had come up with a figure that we thought we could handle—$20,000. This figure represents the bail bond we were prepared to post. Money that would secure Takodah's release until trial, provided he followed all the court's conditions. Still, a lot of money for us to raise.

At the first bail hearing, they didn't bring Takodah to the phone. I was so disheartened and had no idea what had happened. It was a beautiful May day, and when I'm disappointed, I tend to withdraw. I went outside and picked weeds in my garden.

Later, I saw that Takodah had actually called. When we did see each other, he said, "I didn't know what had happened. The guards didn't bring me to the area where I could be on the phone." Major mom guilt. I hadn't answered his phone call to explain. Instead, I hid in my seclusion. My son couldn't contact me. I let him know that we had been waiting, but they couldn't wait any longer, and it had been rescheduled for next week.

We had the hearing, and the judge listened to our proposal. We had already sent it to the lawyer so the court would have it on file, and the lawyer also had a copy at hand when we got on the call.

The judge asked my mom and me some questions about what would happen if Takodah went out of the twenty-five-foot boundary—would we call the police and turn him in? We both were adamant that we would. That we would keep those boundaries in place.

Despite our best efforts and intentions, the judge refused, and Takodah had to stay in jail.

Takodah and I reflected a few times about what would have actually happened had he been granted bail. He confided that he knew he would have messed up if he had been out. By that point, he had been in jail for five months, but truthfully, he was still trying to find a way out and make this all go away. He was still in denial.

Not Released, But Transformed

As the weeks and months went by, I watched Takodah move from survival mode to surrender. He began to lead Bible studies with other men inside. He began quoting scripture to me. I watched him encourage others, forgive himself, and dream again.

And I realized: if God had answered my prayer for his early release, he might have missed this season of transformation.

Because bail was denied, the next best option seemed to be moving him out of *administrative segregation*—a type of isolation where he had little interaction with anyone—into the *general population*, where inmates lived and worked more communally. At first, Takodah was drawn to the idea. He wanted more interaction, more freedom, and had the desire to work in the kitchen.

Takodah thought he was ready. He felt his daily Bible reading and studies with me had prepared him to move on. But before the move was approved, his parole officer looked more closely at what it would mean. He explained the risks that came with general population—the temptations, the conflicts, the easy access to trouble. Through those conversations, Takodah began to see the potential dangers for himself. In the end, he withdrew his request.

I used to think that unanswered prayers meant silence or punishment. But I now believe they're often the deepest acts of love. If Takodah had been released when we asked, he might have walked straight into temptation. That "no" from the judge changed everything. Sometimes protection looks like disappointment until time reveals its purpose.

Entering the TLC Program

In March 2023, I first heard about TLC—Transformational Living Community—from an inmate's wife. I didn't understand what it was at first, but then a chaplain mentioned it to Takodah. The TLC program is located in a different part of the jail—the East Building—and requires a whole new set of routines for both inmates and their visitors. It's a privilege-based, in-prison, 12–18-month structured, faith-based residential program for individuals serious about changing their lives through God's intervention and grace.

While we were learning about the TLC program, I decided I needed a more secure job since my Airbnbs weren't covering all the bills. I had hoped to continue on with the Senior Center, but the month-long training working as a Member Service Center Representative did not work. On March 6, 2023, I began working as a credit union member service center representative, taking phone calls.

The TLC core focus areas include discipleship, spiritual formation, community building, moral and character development, overcoming life-controlling problems, inner healing, family and parenting, coping with incarceration, changing criminal mentality, social adjustment, and education. It's run by Alaska Correctional Ministries, a non-profit that has partnered with the Department of Corrections Chaplaincy Ministry since 1980.

Takodah applied—and was accepted in April 2023.

Guess how I found out? Yup, the Securus message was different. When Takodah called, he was so thrilled.

"Mom, you can actually touch the other inmates!"
The things we take for granted—and sometimes take away from others to punish them—are the most cherished inside.

As usual, with a new program came new procedures. Visits were now in the East Building, and the system was completely different. You couldn't enter the waiting area until 6:15 p.m. Firstly, this allowed the correctional officers time to transition during their 6:00 p.m. shift change, and secondly, it eliminated the need to show up two hours early to get a spot, which had been the norm on the West side. Now, you signed up one hour before the visit and could go back to your car to prepare.

That's exactly what I did. I used that time to reflect, pray, and prepare that night's Daily Bread message and a scripture for our Bible reading together.

Another big change was the program schedule, which consisted of classes from 8:00 a.m. to 4:00 p.m.

TLC WEEKLY SCHEDULE

MONDAY Sept 30	TUESDAY October 1	WEDNESDAY October 2	THURSDAY October 3	FRIDAY October 4	SATURDAY October 5	SUNDAY October 6
8:00 am Morning Devotions	8:00 am Morning Devotions	8:00 am Morning Devotions	7:40 am Morning Devotions	8:00 am Morning Devotions		
8:50 am Ray VanderLaan Vol. 3 Video 1 (Isaiah S.)	8:50 am ADM Dev: Chris H.	8:50 am Family Prayer Dev: David Guthrie.	8:25 am Clean Up & Inspection	8:50 am ADM Dev: Robert G.		
9:45 am Search For Significance Test (Zachary O.)	9:45 am Accept your Calling Video 2 (Brenden M.)	9:45 am The Basics Of Righteousness Video 6 (Paul B.)	9:30 am Bishop Mel's Class Lesson 20 (Bishop Mel)	9:45 am Galatians Video 7 (Brenden M.)		
12:00 pm American Heritage Video 12 (Takodah V.)	12:00 pm Development Group (Chris H.)	12:00 pm Living As An Overcomer Video 1 (Takodah V.)	12:00 pm Cloverhill Prayer Video 3 (William M.)	12:00 pm Love Of God Video 6 (Johnathan H.)		12:00 pm Church Service Miguel G.
1:05 pm At The Altar Of Sexual Idolatry Session 7 (Miguel G.)	1:35 pm Under Cover Video 7 (William M.)	1:20 pm Is Genesis History Movie(1st half) (Frank C.)	1:35 pm Conquer Series Video 4 (Christian R.)	1:20 pm Anger Resolution Lesson 5 Video 3 (2nd Half) (Jeremy D.)		
2:45 pm Not a Fan Video (Damen A.)	2:45 pm Accountability Group/ODM	2:45 pm ODM	2:45 pm Accountability Group/ODM	2:45 pm Mountain of Fire Video (Christian R.)		

That meant no more morning or afternoon visits—just evenings. Thankfully, evenings had already been my usual routine. Friday nights were movie nights, and I could often hear the movie clearly in the background when Takodah came through the heavy door for our visit.

For the first couple of months, he could bring his Bible with him to our visit. I wasn't allowed to carry anything in, but a small note managed to make it through a few times. Then, on one visit, he walked in empty-handed. I never did find out why the rule changed. But I've learned to readjust whenever things change. Just like on the outside, rule changes inside are usually the result of someone abusing a privilege.

As I watched Takodah settle into the TLC routine, something else changed—his heart. In May 2023, he told me he had given his life to Jesus.

That call left me speechless. Not because I didn't believe him—but because I did. His voice was different. Steady. Soft. Full of hope.

After everything we'd been through, this moment wasn't just a turning point. It was a resurrection. He wasn't released from jail, but he was released from the darkness that had wrapped itself around his life. And even though bars still surrounded him, I could finally see light breaking through.

Impact of Transformational Living Community Program (TLC)

I later learned just how respected the TLC Program is—not just inside the walls, but across the state. Chaplain Rudy Bosley, the executive director of the Anchorage Correctional Ministry, shared that the program is supported by the superintendent of the Anchorage Correctional Complex, assistant superintendents, mental health professionals, state and federal attorneys, judges, and even our lieutenant governor, Nancy Dahlstrom. That level of backing says a lot about its impact.

While Alaska has the highest recidivism rate in the country—DOC data shows that 60 percent of released inmates return to jail within three years, and 60 percent of those come back within just 3–6 months—the TLC Program stands out. It has a *68 percent success rate* for graduates who stay out of jail for *at least five years.* Those numbers are a big deal. Real transformation is happening.

When Takodah entered TLC, I didn't know all this yet. I just knew I saw a change in him. Now I understand: he was stepping into a proven space of hope. This program works, and every Alaska prison could benefit from it greatly.

To read more about this program go to https://www.godinprison.com/[12]

Baptism

At the same time, I was on my own spiritual journey. I had always loved church and reading the Bible, but I hadn't fully surrendered to its teachings. In August 2023, after a service, a young woman asked me, "Do you follow Jesus?"
I answered honestly. "Yes. I've finally decided to give my life to the Lord."

She shared her story—how she'd grown up in church, was baptized as a child, drifted away, and later came back. I realized I had done the same. I was baptized during my first marriage and thought I had surrendered, but

I hadn't walked the walk. So I signed up for the baptism class at Anchorage Baptist Temple.

I signed up for the baptism preparation class at Anchorage Baptist Temple, a course designed to guide participants through what it means to publicly commit their lives to Christ and understand the significance of baptism. I took the class on September 24, 2023.

I was so excited—nervous too, but mostly excited—to take this public step of faith. For me, it wasn't just about the class material. It was about standing up and saying, "Yes, I belong to Jesus now." It was about obeying His words: *"Go and make disciples of all nations, baptizing them in the name of the Father and of the Son and of the Holy Spirit"* (Matthew 28:19).[13]

Around that same time, Takodah mentioned they were planning a baptism inside the jail. I had never even heard of something like that happening before, so I was thrilled. He could be baptized, too.

And wouldn't you know—*we were baptized on the same day. November 5, 2023.* We didn't plan it that way—but God did.

As I grew in my faith, I stopped drinking. It wasn't a conscious decision—it just happened. That's the beauty of walking with the Holy Spirit. When you're filled with His presence, other things get pushed out organically. I also noticed I no longer enjoyed certain TV shows. It reminded me of something Darren Hardy said: "What you allow informs your thoughts, behaviors, and habits." You need to flush out the world's beliefs with the Word of God. The more I read Scripture, the more my mind changed—and so did my habits.

At one point, I even found myself a little envious of all the time Takodah had to study the Bible. He'd tell me about the deep classes they were doing inside TLC, and it inspired me. That's why I enrolled in the *Faith Bible Institute* (htttps://fbiclass.com/)[14], a three-year Bible study program built on three key truths:

1. Jesus commanded us to live "by every word." (Matthew 4:4).

2. Spiritual growth comes through the Word. (1 Peter 2:2).

3. The Great Commission commands churches to teach every member "all things" Christ has commanded. (Matthew 28:19–20).

So, in a way, even though he was incarcerated and I was free—we were both students of the Word. We were both being changed, shaped, and stretched in our own TLC journeys: one behind bars, one in the pews.

The deepest truth I've learned in this journey is this: connection with God transforms every other connection in our lives. When I gave my life fully to Christ, I found the peace I'd spent years searching for in people, places, and performance. My son and I don't walk in shame anymore—we walk in grace. And now, I know the only legacy I want to leave behind is one built on faith, not fear.

Chapter Six
The Weight We Carry

20 The one who sins is the one who will die. The child will not share the guilt of the parent, nor will the parent share the guilt of the child. The righteousness of the righteous will be credited to them, and the wickedness of the wicked will be charged against them.

Ezekiel 18:20 [15]

Even in the midst of joy and spiritual breakthroughs, life does not pause for reflection. Faith does not mean an absence of grief, guilt, or fear. It simply gives us a framework to face them with grace. Just as the waves of transformation carry us forward, the waves of challenge crash against us, reminding us that growth and pain are intertwined. My journey with God—and with Takodah—taught me that every stage of grief, every pang of guilt, and every moment of fear connects to the larger process of healing and hope.

Having your child arrested is one of the most demanding situations imaginable.

There is grief that comes when your child is incarcerated. But layered over that grief is guilt—heavy, accusing, persistent.

Some days I thought:

Where did I go wrong?

What should I have done differently?

Why didn't I see the signs?

What kind of mother am I that my child is in jail, charged with murder?

These aren't questions people ask you directly, but they're the questions you hear in your own head. And sometimes in the silence of others.

In January of 2021, I joined the first-ever group to go through Darren Hardy's *Hero's Journey* program. In the workbook, he shares: "A hero is simply an ordinary person put in an extraordinary circumstance who takes action."[16]

That quote never left me, especially after my son was arrested.

Later in the same workbook, another line struck me deeply:

"You have a hero inside. You need only to awaken it. You need to create demanding situations that summon the greatness inside."[16]

A loved one being arrested is a demanding situation.

Takodah's dad first asked, "What could I have done differently? What did I do wrong?"

I asked myself those same questions. But my first, rawest question was different: "What could have made Takodah so mad that he'd end up in a position where he wanted to hurt somebody—never mind killing them?"

I believe I approached it from that angle because of the personal development work I'd done over the years. I had taken many courses, driven by my dream of becoming an entrepreneur and starting a business. Those classes taught me to look inward, to reflect on the past so I could shape a better future. That mindset shaped how I processed everything.

Takodah's dad, on the other hand, grew up on a farm. Both of his grandparents had large working farms. His approach was grounded in action: you do something, learn what works and what doesn't, and keep moving forward. He learned by doing. I learned by reading and reflecting. And when the worst happened, our internal wiring led us down two very different paths in trying to understand what had gone wrong.

Both approaches had value, but I share this because I know that parents will grieve and process trauma differently. There's no right way—just your way, and what leads you toward truth and healing.

Guilt and Shame

Guilt and shame are two of the hardest weights a parent can carry—especially when your child is incarcerated. After Takodah was arrested, I reflected on messages from his friend months before, saying he was using meth. I remembered the denial from him at Thanksgiving. Were drugs the root cause of this nightmare? Was this event proof of his lying?

According to Wikipedia, *guilt* is an emotional experience that occurs when a person believes or realizes—accurately or not—that they have compromised their own standards of conduct or have violated a moral standard and bear significant responsibility for that violation. That described exactly how I felt as a mother.

But guilt wasn't acting alone. *Shame*, as defined in the same article, is the painful feeling arising from the consciousness of something dishonorable or improper done by oneself or another. It lingers differently than guilt—it's less about what I did and more about who I thought I was. It was about my identity, not my actions. I began believing I was a bad parent.

In 2022, I had already started confronting this lie. On the drive home from visiting Takodah, I listened to *The Four Agreements* audiobook again. It had become my companion in the car, comforting me even before his imprisonment, during that long drive home after seeing Takodah for the last time outside the bars. Now, the book reminded me that as children, we are often told things—truths we had no power to question or reject. We didn't know we had a choice. But as adults, we get to choose. We don't have to keep agreeing with the "truths" that were handed down to us. One line gripped me: Don't believe the lies you tell yourself. That was the moment I chose to stop agreeing with the lie that I was a bad mom.

One of the most healing steps came during a visit after Takodah had moved into the TLC program in 2023. Through tears, I asked him, "Did you feel abandoned when I moved to Anchorage back in 2010?"

He didn't hesitate: "I knew it was a hard, needed choice."

Even though I had second-guessed that decision for years, that moment gave me peace. I had carried the weight of our family's breakup in the same way I carried my parents' divorce—as a wound of disconnection. But I saw clearly then: this cycle of brokenness didn't have to continue. With our growing faith, I realized—and told Takodah—we could end it right here, with us.

I used to believe my story was too "vanilla"—not dramatic enough, not inspiring enough. But reading the Bible showed me that God uses ordinary people for extraordinary purposes. Why not me?

Think about who God chooses in Scripture:

Rahab, a prostitute, hid the Israelite spies and became part of the lineage of Jesus.

David, a young shepherd boy and later an adulterer and murderer, became a man after

God's own heart.

Matthew, a despised tax collector, was chosen as one of Jesus' disciples.

I'm just a mom who loves her son—but so were many of the women in the Bible. They were mothers, daughters, caregivers, and leaders. God didn't wait for them to be perfect. He used their willingness.

That gave me hope. My letters with Takodah began changing. Instead of just venting our worries or sharing daily updates, we began seeking Christ together. We started praying about breaking generational cycles. We wanted to raise the next generation—his future children—differently.

We came across this Scripture, and it stopped us both:

> *"Honor your father and mother"—which is the first commandment with a promise—"so that it may go well with you and that you may enjoy long life on the earth." —Ephesians 6:2-3* [17]

That verse struck something in both of us. It wasn't about perfect parenting or perfect children. It was about honor—restoring it, receiving it, offering it.

As faith builds, you begin to see your life's purpose beyond personal pain. I began to understand that the pain I had carried—guilt from the past, shame over my parenting, fear about Takodah's future—could all be used for something holy.

Recently, while talking to one of my early trusted accountability partners from Darren Hardy's *Hero's Journey* program, she gently pointed out that I always referred to Takodah as a "person of interest" but never said more.

I had told the *Hero's Journey* group I was facilitating that I couldn't lead that Saturday, just ten days before he became a person of interest. But when my world flipped upside down, I stayed silent. Leading this group was already a stretch for me, and admitting my son was a person of interest felt like failure—who was I to lead? And then, when they found his car abandoned, no communication with him, realizing he was on the run—who can admit that to people you have only met over Zoom?

That's why the first people I truly opened up to were my personal accountability partners—women I had actually met in person. There was trust there, and I needed that safety before I could be fully honest. Even then,

I was very guarded. I didn't want questions or judgment—I just needed them to know that my life was in upheaval.

It took me a couple of weeks to even bring it up with the people who were supposed to walk beside me. You'd think your accountability partners would be the first people you turn to, but I hesitated. Deep down, I was afraid of judgment—not just for my son's actions, but for mine. I imagined their thoughts: How could you let this happen? What kind of mother were you? Those were the questions already tormenting me, and I wasn't ready to hear them from anyone else.

My friend Rhonda, whom I met in 2024 at the Anchorage Correctional Complex, went through something similar. As she prepared a speech for our 2025 Alaska Correctional Ministries annual fundraiser, she shared that she had completely isolated herself in the beginning—only able to talk to people she knew she could trust one hundred percent. She didn't understand why it had happened to her son, and she couldn't bear to believe that he might actually be guilty. Even after a year of not connecting with her immediate family, when she did finally reunite with them, she didn't talk about her son Jeremy at all. Everyone just pretended he didn't exist—because speaking his name meant facing the impossible.

I, too, can pinpoint denial on my journey. Looking back to October, before everything happened, someone told me Takodah might be into drugs. Then came Thanksgiving, and his behavior felt off. He ate, slept, and ate some more, barely said a word to anyone. But I always want to think the best of people—especially my children. At that point, I wasn't ready to consider the possibility that he might be using drugs. Maybe it was naïveté.

Maybe it was protective hope. But when he was officially labeled a person of interest, I realised how utterly unprepared I truly was.

To this day, I struggle to say the word murder. It doesn't matter that Takodah admitted what he did. It doesn't matter that he found the Lord and is transforming his life from the inside out. He took a life, and society defines him by that act. At first, I couldn't bring myself to speak of the crime he was accused of—such a horrendous crime. It felt too horrific to say aloud.

Recently, I read something Takodah wrote in September 2024: a sermon that shifted something deep inside me. It read:

A brother said to me once that the depth of my conviction for God was due to the depth of my criminal conviction. There is a great amount of truth in that. While I hate how much sin it took to get my attention, I know there's nothing else that would have shown me my deep need for Jesus.

If I had come in on any lesser charges, I would have been hanging out with all the people I knew in the Fairbanks jail, getting deeper into the lifestyle I had been living, pushing the people who love me further away, and causing more hurt and pain to those around me.

God knew it would take looking at a life sentence and being thrown into a cell alone to snap me out of the life I was immersed in. When I think of Jesus dying so that I can have life, I'm struck by how real that is. I know exactly what it means for the cost of my life to be paid by the loss of another. Sometimes it leaves me full of questions about why He chose to spare and save me, but ultimately all I can do is be thankful and love God with everything that I am.

This whole thought and reflection came about through the story of a sinful woman and the parable of two debtors found in Luke 7.

After reading this, I realized that in 2024, I had overlooked his admission—that he needed this complete brokenness to be transformed. I see now that God was working from day one. This is also a testament to the incredible transformation the TLC program facilitates. Takodah had to study Scripture and reflect deeply to write such a heartfelt sermon.

One of the most powerful lessons I've learned is this: talk to your loved one about your struggles. Your fears and feelings will shift over time—whether they've just been arrested, are in a pre-sentencing facility, or have moved into a sentenced facility. As they learn and grow, so will you.

These conversations can be healing. Just recently—ninety-nine days into his prison sentence—I told Takodah that I still struggle to say the word murder. He didn't judge me. Instead, he shared how his understanding of Christian maturity continues to develop. That exchange reminded me that we're not meant to carry this weight alone.

We talked about how God sees us as His children—completely made new, not just in our actions, but in our hearts, our thoughts, our identity. We are called to become more like the perfect, sinless Jesus Christ who died for us.

Today, I do not see Takodah as a convicted murderer, even though that is what put him in prison.

Today, I see him for who he is: a disciple of Jesus Christ.

And I am, too.

Chapter Seven

Early Transfer

5 Trust in the Lord with all your heart And lean not on your own understanding; 6 In all your ways submit to him, And he will make your paths straight.

Proverbs 3:5–6 [18]

I turned the calendar to March 2025. There it was—March 17, circled in black ink. At the November 2024 Change of Plea hearing, the judge had stated Takodah needed to be in Fairbanks by that date. Since Fairbanks was where the crime happened, the final sentencing hearing had to be there. Now, seeing it in black and white, there was no more avoiding the truth. No more pretending we had time.

So why was I caught off guard when I missed that call on a Friday afternoon, March 7? We had been preparing for this moment. We knew it was coming. And yet, when it arrived, it landed like a gut punch. In my mind, we had until March 13 or 14—the 7th wasn't even on my radar.

I enjoy working from home on Fridays, as my Member Service Center employer allowed us and furnished all the equipment to work from home, surrounded by my dogs and able to check in with my husband during breaks. I rarely worried about glancing at my phone between work calls or checking messages. But that Friday, as my phone lit up with an incoming call, something felt off. The number was familiar yet strange—not from the usual Anchorage Correctional. My heart skipped a beat.

I was with a customer. I couldn't answer. But deep down, I knew. Takodah was gone.

I had planned to see him that night—to look into his eyes one last time before his transfer, to remind him how much I loved him—but that moment had been stolen from me. I thought I had until next Thursday at the earliest.

The call had come at 2:30 p.m., but I had to wait until 3:00 p.m. to get out of work before I could get to the bottom of that strangely familiar missed call.

When I finally checked, the automated voice confirmed my worst fear: *You missed a call from an incarcerated individual at Fairbanks Correctional Center.*

Hearing it made it real. Yet somehow, my mind still struggled to grasp it.

When shock hits, I lean on the tools I've built—the resilience, the faith, the support system. I texted Chaplain Bryan, my steady source of guidance since this journey began:

"Is Takodah gone? I got a missed call from Fairbanks Correctional Facility."

No response.

Next, I texted Takodah's dad:
"Takodah is in Fairbanks."

His reply was immediate:
"Thanks, he called a bit ago."

My heart clenched. Why didn't he tell me? Why did I have to be the one who updates everyone? I wanted to lash out, demand why I had to find out this way. But I swallowed my frustration and forced my fingers to type a calm response:
"I missed his call. Please keep me updated."

"Will do. We just hung up. They flew him up there."

Flew him? That thought had never crossed my mind. I had assumed he would be transported by van, the way Chaplain Bryan once described. The realization sent another wave of emotions crashing over me.

I immediately texted my mom:
"Takodah's in Fairbanks."

Her response was instant:
"What?"

"They flew him up today," I answered.

"Why so soon?" she asked.

We'd known he had to be there by March 17th, but this early transfer caught us both off guard.

"Yes, I missed his call, but his dad spoke to him," I replied.

Mom called almost immediately. She asked again why so soon. I could hear the strain in her voice, the way she was reaching for something—anything—positive in this moment.

"I know there is good in every event," she said, "but I'm struggling with this one."

I sighed. I wanted to tell her I was struggling, too. Instead, I offered what little comfort I could: "He's been ready. We were hoping for next week, but now you have an opening in your schedule tomorrow."

She chuckled softly at the thought. "Now we can do things together," she said. It was a small consolation. She had been visiting him every Saturday, usually by herself. The routine would be gone now. But we ended the call with a quiet understanding: We would stay in touch by text and share any updates.

As I processed everything, my daughter texted me:
"Hi. Takodah tried to call you, but the phone wouldn't let him. He also wants Chaplain Rudy's phone number."

Another pang of guilt. He had tried to reach me first. I was supposed to be the first voice he heard, the first reassurance. But he had gone down his list—his dad, then his sister. Still, I found comfort in knowing he had people to call. Communication was everything in moments like this.

And so we waited. My husband sat to my left, my retired sled dog curled up to my right. The weight of silence pressed down on me. At 4:00 p.m., my phone rang again.

This time, I was ready.

I fumbled through setting up my Securus account, which I had let go unfunded while he was in Anchorage; the tedious prompts stretched the moment unbearably. I knew Takodah was on the other end, waiting. Wondering. Hoping. Finally, I pressed one to accept the call.

"Hi, Takodah," I said, exhaling.

"Hi, Mom," he replied.

Relief flooded me.

I asked him how it all happened. Was the mod able to pray over you? He told me they had called his name over the intercom at 7:00 a.m.: *"Takodah *****, roll up."*

They'd been in lockdown since 1 p.m. the day before. Lockdowns can happen for a number of reasons: inmate fights, Correctional Officers (COs) responding to an overdose, or other medical emergencies. During a lockdown, all inmates must return to their cells, keeping both them and the COs safe. With the inmates contained, officers can focus on the event. Unfortunately, no time for goodbyes. No final prayers with his mod. Thankfully, his cellmate and mentor was able to pray with him. Overall, he just had time to grab his things and go.

I understand the need for "no prior knowledge" of when they will be moved. I empathize with him and the pain he must have felt. The men in the Transitional Living Community (TLC) program had become family. They had seen his pain and triumphs.

"Chaplain Bryan gave me a packet of your papers last night," I told him. "That must have meant you were ready to leave."

He chuckled softly, but there was something distant in his voice. "I gave those to him a month ago."

"So, you flew the coop, huh?" I joked, trying to lighten the moment.

He hesitated. Maybe it was too soon. Instead, he told me about the flight:

"There were four of us. I sat and looked out at the tarmac through the big windows; it was so big. It wasn't just the small square I've been looking out at for the past two years. On the flight, I saw mountains, sky, clouds—just incredible."

After two years inside, he had finally seen the world beyond concrete walls—freedom, in a way, even if only through a window at 30,000 feet in the air.

"Where are you now?" I asked.

"I'm in F-Mod."

"Do you have a cellmate?"

"It's just cots in an open area. No cells. Five or seven of us here. No privacy."

That would be an adjustment. He had never lived in that situation before. It reminded me of a friend whose grandson, incarcerated in Fairbanks, had gone to work, and all his stuff was stolen. I didn't want that for my son.

"I've been doing a lot of praying," he admitted.

"That's what you've been preparing for," I reminded him.

He hesitated. "On the drive to the airport, I shared a little. I'm waiting for the right opportunity to share."

"Listen first," I felt compelled to tell him. "Understand what people need before you speak."

I know that guidance came from going to our weekly family support group and studying my Bible. To listen is to hear the Holy Spirit's prompting.

"My dear brothers and sisters, take note of this: Everyone should be quick to listen, slow to speak and slow to become angry." —James 1:19 (NIV)[19]

"Yeah," he agreed. "I've been doing a lot of listening and praying."

That awareness—it was growth, it was change. It was exactly what I had prayed for.

We sat in awkward silence before he asked, "Are you okay?"

I smiled. "I really am. Because I have God. And so do you. You are not alone."

Near the end of the conversation, he asked, "How often do you want me to call?"

Wow, I thought to myself. Three years ago, I begged for phone calls. Now, he was offering them freely. My heart overflowed; tears rolled down my face. As you go through each transition, you will realize there is growth—be open to see it.

"Every day. Tomorrow is open. Sunday, I'll be at church, but other than that, call whenever you can. Remember, I get off work at 3 p.m."

"There's no clock here," he mused. "Hopefully, I can get one from the commissary."

Time. Such a simple thing, something we take for granted. Now, for him, it was a void to be filled. In TLC, they had a daily and weekly schedule. For the moment, he was in a void, and only he could decide how to fill it.

This was when I felt the most hopeless. I couldn't help; I couldn't just visit and fill the void.

When the call ended, I sat still, absorbing the weight of this transition. Takodah was prepared. I was prepared. But that didn't make it easy. We had prayed, we had hoped, and now, the moment had come. Would he rise to the occasion, or would the weight of his past pull him under?

This was Takodah's moment of trial, his crucible—the ordeal that would test his courage and faith.

Growth is rarely a straight path. There will be moments of hesitation, moments when fear whispers louder than faith. But even in those moments, the foundation has been raised. Even when you shrink back, you are stronger than before. And just like every challenge, we would face it together—one day, one prayer, one phone call at a time.

Chapter Eight
Sentencing

Don't be misled—you cannot mock the justice of God. You will always harvest what you plant.
Galatians 6:7 [20]

March 24, 2025: Monday—the day had finally arrived. I had driven up a week before, thankfully able to work out of the Fairbanks office. My mom and her partner flew up Sat.

We had just celebrated my mom's eighty-second birthday on Saturday. We even talked to Takodah and asked where we should go for her birthday dinner. His suggestion was a charming Italian restaurant with impressive tall, sturdy tables and high chairs—perfect for her birthday, since my mom has always been drawn to high tables.

On Sunday, I had picked up my husband from the airport. When we got to the hotel room, he mentioned he hadn't figured out the Fairbanks visitor form yet. I was surprised—he has such an amazing mind, able to visualize things in three dimensions and project them mentally. Unfortunately, this meant he couldn't visit Takodah that day.

Earlier that morning, my mom, her partner, and I had gone to visit Takodah at 9:00 a.m., only to find a sign saying "No visits." That sign is always disheartening—you build up anticipation, then it's dashed with no explanation. So, my mom and I decided to visit a local church instead. The sermon was wonderful, centered around Zacchaeus climbing a tree to see Jesus.

After the service, I spoke with the pastor about their prison ministry. He said they would be holding an Easter service—the first one since the end of COVID. The jail had hoped that all local churches could coordinate and participate, but that proved too complicated. He was thrilled they got the go-ahead just for Easter.

While I was picking up my husband, my mom's partner called the jail and found out visits were allowed at 2:00 p.m. Unfortunately, they didn't have a car, and the text alert took too long to reach me, so they weren't able to go. Tensions were a little high, but we decided to have dinner together before heading to Takodah's 8:30 p.m. visit time.

I hadn't told Takodah that my mom's partner was on the visitor list. Mom and I were so hopeful he could—or would—wait the hour while we visited. Gloriously, all three of us were able to see him. We talked about whether he felt ready for sentencing. He was looking forward to wearing real clothes—a button-down shirt, slacks, a tie, belt, vest, and nice shoes. We talked about Mom's birthday, the dinner, the church service, and that his stepdad had flown first class.

Talking before sentencing was helpful: it allowed everyone to see each other before being in court, where we would have zero control. Quietly,

"Love you" was exchanged. Afterward, we watched Takodah leave with a somber nod, and we headed back to the hotel.

I set the alarm for 7:00 a.m. We planned to meet Takodah's stepmom and the father of a childhood friend at the courthouse at 1:30 p.m. Sentencing would begin at 2:00 p.m.

We all had breakfast in the hotel's open banquet room. Afterward, I found a small shop that sold pocket-sized Kleenex. I took a picture of two pouches and posted it on social media with this caption:

"If there is any day I need Kleenex, it's today. Keep praying. #prayerworks #prayers. I know I need my prayer warriors to stand in for me and my family. I am so thankful I have a network, and I'm going to use it."

Thirty people reacted. It was one of my most engaging posts.

We drove downtown—a quick five-minute drive, but too long a walk for my mom. We parked at a two-hour spot. We had to walk through an X-ray machine, similar to those at the airport and put our phones and keys on the conveyor belt.

I knew where Room 407 was, so I led the way. There was a crowd—more people than I expected.

I saw Takodah's stepmom talking to a lady who was a juror for another case. I was relieved—this was supposed to be an intimate proceeding. Nearby, an older lady was holding a poster board of pictures. Four or five others were milling about. They were all waiting for the same door to open.

The anticipation in my body grew.

We filed into the courtroom; the family of the deceased to the left, us to the right. My husband went in first, entering the third row, followed by me and Takodah's stepmom. Our friend's dad took the back row. I was surprised to see my mom and her partner go to the front row.

I tried not to glance to my left. They must be hurting so much today—to finally face the person responsible for their loved one's death.

I looked ahead and noticed a young boy wandering—the four-year-old who had lost his father. Waiting for my son to arrive, I wondered what would happen. Would the judge hear my son's heart and recognize how much he had changed?

Then I heard the metal door open to my right. This must be him.

Shock. It was Takodah—but he was wearing the yellow prison clothes.

Immediately, I thought: How disappointed he must be. Then: Where did the communication break down? The paralegal had assured him his clothes would be ready.

Seconds passed by, but my heart was heavy with unease.

The public defender came in and sat next to Takodah. They whispered quietly. Then the district attorney entered, greeted the victim's family, and opened her laptop. The judge followed.

I fully expected someone to say, "All rise," but no one did. Too many TV courtroom dramas had run through my mind.

The judge began by stating the charges against Takodah—the cold, hard statement. Yes. This is why we were here. The words echoed in my head again and again.

The District Attorney (DA) and public defender updated the court on whether anything had changed since the plea deal.

The DA stated the 30-year sentence was within the agreed terms and that the state was satisfied it would keep others safe.

The public defender said the sentence should be viewed as rehabilitation time. They believed thirty years with ten suspended and seven years for assault, two years concurrent, would allow for behavioral evaluation and rehabilitation.

He acknowledged the heinous act and Takodah's part and stated he believed the length was prudent.

Then the judge said the DA had informed him that family members wanted to say a few words. They were welcome to approach the witness stand or speak into a microphone in the pews.

I wasn't prepared for this. I sat bracing for what they would say about my son—the adult in that courtroom was not the young man I knew.

The aunt who first spoke brought the poster board of pictures. She said she had been to every hearing except one and that her nephew's name had never been spoken—not once. But she was going to say his name now: Lee ***.

That struck me. His name had been invisible in the proceedings, while my son's name was mentioned at every hearing. Both sides felt the weight of it. Everyone knew my son's name, read his name and articles, while Lee's had remained almost hidden.

It was profound to think about their pain.

Another aunt spoke about the deceased—that he wasn't perfect, swinging between joy and despair, freedom and incarceration, love and anger. And that they would never know his full potential, and that his son would never know his love.

She said she was now an elder and that holding grudges was not in her character.

Turning to Takodah, she said, "I don't know what you will turn out to be, but I forgive you. Use this time to reflect." As she spoke, I thought, *here is God's grace in action.*

Gratitude quickly turned to renewed sorrow when the next woman spoke.

She introduced herself as a family friend and said, "I am also an elder. I cannot forgive you. I believe you should get the same sentence as Lee's death." Listening to these women, I hurt for them—I could feel the depth of the beauty that had been stolen.

At the same time, I thought of the continued harm my son's drug dealing, anger, and pride might have caused had he not ended up in jail.

His crime was heinous. I hate the crime he committed.

But I will forever be thankful for the spiritual growth he has undergone since his incarceration.

After family and friends spoke, the judge surprised us by saying the defendant's family wanted to say a few words.

In my head, I thought, "What? I haven't prepared anything."

The judge had received letters of support from me and other family members.

I think he saw my confusion.

He continued by saying he believed someone was on the phone—Chaplain Rudy.

Yes, of course, Chaplain Rudy, executive director of the Alaska Correctional Ministry and head of the TLC program, and a mentor of mine.

Chaplain Rudy spoke about the program he had guided Takodah through, highlighting the reduced recidivism of inmates who go through TLC.

The words that stood out to me were:

"I met Takodah as a broken young man. He came in angry and hurting. He applied himself to learn about his anger and where it came from. This is not an easy program. They have four classes every day, homework, and accountability. He didn't just check boxes and get things done. He looked into himself. He wanted change and moved up in responsibility."

I don't know if the family and friends could hear—or take in—those words. I can only imagine their hurt. But I know the change I've gone through and the change I've seen in my son.

Takodah was allowed to speak to the court.

He had prepared bullet points of what he wanted to say.

He began by taking full responsibility for his actions. He acknowledged that anger and drugs had been involved, but emphasised that this was no excuse.

His actions were done without thought of the consequences.

"I am so sorry for your loss."

Tears welled in his eyes.

Judge Bennett's final words were:

"I don't know what will become of you—that is up to you. I can see you have put in the work, not just checked off the boxes."

After the hearing, a police officer explained to Takodah how to press his fingers on the fingerprint card. His hands were cuffed in front of him. Takodah pressed his fingers and was ushered out.

The family and friends had left.

The public defender introduced himself to us—an odd feeling to meet the person who had talked to my son about his crime.

We asked about the clothes. The judge had said civilian clothes were only for trial.

Afterward, in the hallway, family and friends mingled.

The older aunt introduced herself to me.

My husband introduced me as Takodah's mom and my mom as his grandmother.

She continued to be gracious, saying she forgave Takodah.

There had been so much loss in the past five years.

They were going to have a potlatch the next day.

She said Lee's son had a good mom and would be raised with happiness.

As we left, it was surreal.

Here I was, leaving with my son's stepmom, hugging her goodbye, knowing we would continue to talk.

I had my husband's support, my mom's presence, and the heavy knowledge of the next chapter of my son's life.

***

The next morning, we went to the jail for a 9:30 a.m. visit.

As I drove, I felt sadness and anger swelling inside of me.

I didn't know what I was going to say exactly.

I knew I could finally ask what really happened.

We all sat down.

His glasses were broken.

He sat and tried to get them to stay together.

It felt like ten minutes, but it was only two.

My first words to my 25-year-old son were: "I'm mad at you, Takodah."

I hadn't let myself say those words in three years.

Tears streamed down my face.

"I'm so sorry, Mom," he replied.

That one word—*Mom*—has brought me to tears countless times.

By the grace of God, I have learned to separate the crime—the sins—from the person.

I've seen the Lord's grace and love at work in both my son and me over these years, shaping us in ways only He could.

We will never stop growing in the Scriptures and sharing our story, discovering healing, accountability and hope.

And through our story, we strive to let others see that transformation is possible, even in the midst of profound brokenness.

Chapter Nine

The Hit

2 Consider it pure joy, my brothers and sisters,[a] whenever you face trials of many kinds, 3 because you know that the testing of your faith produces perseverance. 4 Let perseverance finish its work so that you may be mature and complete, not lacking anything.

James 1:2–4 [21]

I wanted to believe the hardest part was over. After sentencing, after asking the questions that haunted us for years, I thought closure might finally come. Instead, another wave was waiting—one I never saw coming.

I thought sentencing and being able to ask openly what happened would be the last major event. It would be closure for both the deceased's family and friends. It would start the healing in ministry for Takodah and for our family.

I guess that was me being naïve again.

After arriving back home on Tuesday night, I woke up to my phone alarm at 5:00 a.m. as usual on Thursday morning. As I headed to the bathroom, I saw I had three missed calls and two waiting text messages. Why were Chaplain Bryan and my friend Rhonda calling at 10:00 p.m.?

I had spoken to Takodah on Wednesday night and knew Chaplain Bryan hadn't been able to visit him. I had actually gone to church to be surrounded by my Christian brothers and sisters and had spoken to the pastor, who refused Chaplain Bryan's request for overtime so he could fly out and see Takodah. He explained that since Bryan is on staff with the church, the pastor could make that decision.

So—the combination of missed calls and text messages, plus knowing Chaplain Bryan was told not to visit, meant something serious was happening.

As I read the message from Chaplain Bryan, my mind was reaching for reasons. I still wasn't prepared for the truth. I don't think we ever really are. What I read shocked me... "Please call me asap" then 20 minutes later: "I'm on the road, driving to check on Takodah. Please call me."

My advice: Establish a network with as many people as possible. Have a group chat so people can see who else is supporting you. Chaplain Bryan knew Rhonda and I were close, so he reached out to her to try to connect with me. Another piece of advice: it is okay to have your phone ringer off. It allowed me to sleep and be rested and ready for the news I was about to receive.

I called Rhonda at 5:00 a.m. I had no idea if she would be awake, but I needed to know what she knew. I had first tried calling Chaplain Bryan, but only got his voicemail. He had said he arrived in Fairbanks at 4:30, so I really wasn't surprised.

"Hi Rhonda," I said.

"What is going on?" I asked with anticipation.

She answered, "Chaplain Bryan asked me to try and call you. He said Takodah was fine."

I asked her specifically, "Is Takodah okay?"

She said, "He's driving up to Fairbanks to check on him."

"Okay, thank you. I pray everything is okay," I replied.

Next, I looked up the facility phone number and dialed, pressing zero for the switchboard.
"Hello, I'm Heidi Sheldon. Is Takodah ***** okay? My chaplain drove up from Anchorage last night to check on him."

The reply was: "If he came in from Anchorage, he's in booking."

"No," I explained, "my chaplain drove up from Anchorage. Takodah is already in Fairbanks jail."

Again, he replied: "If he came in last night, then he is still in booking."

I tried one more time. "No, Takodah ***** was sentenced on Monday. He is in S2 mod. Were there any fights last night? I'm trying to find out if he is okay."

The reply: "There were no disturbances in S2 last night."

"Thank you for this information," I said, and hung up.

You may feel frustrated at times. But yelling at the guard who answers the phone won't get quicker answers. They're just doing their job, and they don't always have the full picture.

Psalm 103:8 [22] *The Lord is merciful and gracious, slow to anger and abounding in love.*
I needed to remember this as I dealt with other people. Especially now, at this time of uncertainty.

This has become a steadfast verse for me.

I encourage you to find an online resource for encouraging words during stressful times. The Bible is my number one resource—it continually gives me calming, reassuring words when I have no other answers.

By 5:00 am, I had gathered as much information as I could. After sentencing, I had carefully noted the visiting hours. The chaplain planned on seeing Takodah at 9:00 a.m., which gave me some reassurance that he was safe. I decided I would call the receptionist at 8:00 a.m. once they had arrived.

Keeping to my schedule and routine is comforting in stressful times. I started heating the kettle for coffee, let the dogs out for their morning pee, and read *My Daily Bread*. After making coffee and reading Takodah and my 365 devotional reading, I took the dogs for their walk.

I used the walk to talk to God:

Lord, I don't know what is going on. But thank you for Chaplain Bryan. Thank you for the officer telling me everything is okay, no incidents last night. Thank you for your protection and for always being there.

Chaplain Bryan called right before 8:00 a.m. "I'm getting ready to see Takodah. He is safe. He called last night and said he felt threatened. He was very careful about how he talked, but they moved him to medical. I'll update you after I see him. I will work on getting him moved."

"Thank you, Chaplain Bryan. Thank you so much for being there for him," I replied.

I then called the receptionist. "Has Takodah ***** been moved?"

The reply: "No." In the background, I could hear other conversations. She seemed distracted. I decided to wait for Chaplain Bryan's call.

But I couldn't just sit around and not look for information. I knew his stepmom was going to visit, so I used Facebook Messenger to ask, "When are you visiting today?"

"9:30 a.m.," came the reply. "Lots of meetings today," I responded. "Oh—Chaplain Bryan was going to be visiting at 9:00 a.m. He drove up last night. He mentioned Takodah might have felt threatened. The front desk didn't say he was in a different mod when I called. I'll share more information when I find out, including with Takodah's dad and my mom. No need to worry them with minimal information. We'll wait for Chaplain Bryan to update me."

Clear communication should always be the goal. Slow down and reread your messages before sending them. At this stage, I was trying to get his step-mom and me on the same page. I found out later that she had informed Takodah's dad once she knew more. In situations like this, coordinating with others is important, but sometimes things don't go as smoothly as we'd like.

I told my husband the little I knew before heading to work at 10:30 a.m. Once I arrived in the parking lot, I reached out after the visit was done. I asked Takodah's stepmom, "Did you visit?"

Her reply: "I did."

I often wonder why I'm not updated promptly, but God has helped me become more patient.

"How is he feeling?" I asked.

Her reply: "Things seemed heavy for him today. He told me everything. I did get him to laugh multiple times, which made me smile."

I probed more. Because I wasn't sure if she meant they talked about being threatened the night before or the events of his crime. "A blessing having you there today. Everything from last night or three years ago?"

Her reply: "All of it. It was a lot to take in. I wish I weren't traveling—I'd like to keep visiting him."

I wanted to know more, but she had already said she had meetings all day. I would have to wait for Chaplain Bryan's call.

At work, I told my manager that the chaplain had gone to Fairbanks to check on Takodah. She immediately said, "Jump off any time if you get a phone call. We'll adjust your adherence."

You may be feeling like you can't share with your boss. You know best. But I wanted my bosses to understand what was going on—to let them know there may be times I'd be distracted. Both managers I've had have been incredible throughout this process.

I had a 15-minute break and a 30-minute lunch, but still no call. My phone was on my desk, silent but ready to be grabbed. Finally, while finishing a call, my phone rang—Chaplain Bryan.

I answered while walking to the breakroom, giving a thumbs-up to my manager. Sitting down, I said, "Okay, I'm sitting down."

"First off," he said, "Takodah is safe and okay. After church services last night, an inmate came up to him and said a friend of the family had contacted inmates to put a hit on him."

Tears came. Blood drained from my head. My stomach clenched. Someone had put a hit on my son. This only happens in other prisons, in group chats—not in real life. Not in mine.

My next thought: *I know the family and friends are hurting, but this goes above and beyond.*

Chaplain Bryan continued: "They moved him into booking last night for his safety. They've now placed him in segregation. He spoke with his Institutional Parole Officer (IPO), and together they filled out the paperwork. Although it may take a week, the IPO agrees that moving him back to Anchorage is the best option. I'm sending an email requesting his return to the TLC program right now."

I don't know if I asked any questions. My mind was in disbelief. He's safe, and they're working on moving him. I sat there stunned, crying, my heart breaking at the thought that people had contacted gang members and put a plan in place.

The consequences of actions ripple out far and wide. My poor son was living the cost in real time.

I called my husband and told him. "Takodah is safe," I began, but the tears came again. "They put a hit out for him. They're trying to get him moved to Anchorage."

Doug gave me a calm, reassuring answer: "I love you."

"I love you," I responded. "I'll see you later."

I then went to tell my manager.

I sat down. My boss asked, "What's going on?"

I replied, "Chaplain Bryan said Takodah is safe, but... they put a hit out on my son."

Tears flowed. Tissues were handed.

"I haven't cried like this in years," I admitted.

"Oh my," she said. "Are they moving him?"

"They're working on it. A friend of the family had said they could not forgive him after the sentencing. It was that friend who ordered the hit, I believe."

"Do you need to take the afternoon off?"

"No," I replied. "There's just an hour left. I'll finish up."

For me, keeping busy is usually best. But each parent will have to find their own rhythm. Sometimes stepping away is needed. Other times, staying the course brings stability.

As I returned to my desk, I whispered a prayer: *Thank you, God, for putting these men in our lives to act quickly. Thank you for protecting my son.*

I knew I had to let my mom know. We'd see each other at 7:00 p.m. at the Beyond Walls support meeting, but this couldn't wait.

At 2:51 p.m., I texted: "You home? Can I come over? I'm done at work at 3:00."

"Yes!" she replied.

As I left work to drive to her house, I thought: *I can't believe what I'm about to tell her. I thought sentencing would be the last stressful thing we'd have to endure.*

No matter where you are in the process—just starting, facing sentencing, or years into serving time—flexibility is key. Acknowledging that we do not have control of the situation can bring peace. As Scripture says, "And which of you by being anxious can add a single hour to his span of life?" (Matthew 6:27) [23]

The two biggest lessons I learned from this moment:

1. Having a network is vital. Try to find a local support group. Join

an online support group. Utilize other moms you meet while visiting. Connection is necessary.

2. Your faith will be tested. For me, this unexpected stress only deepened my reliance on God. From the moment I saw the missed call to the moment I shared at the Thursday night support group, I knew my son and I were in His hands.

Deuteronomy 31:6[24] reminds us, "Be strong and courageous. Do not fear or be in dread of them, for it is the Lord your God who goes with you. He will not leave you or forsake you." I truly felt that in this moment. Looking back, it only confirmed how dependent I am on God and that He never forsakes me.

As terrifying as it was to know someone wanted to kill my son, I am thankful he was moved. I am thankful the chaplains acted quickly. I am thankful he was kept safe.

But I also knew there was more waiting. How quickly would they move him to Anchorage? Each day reminded me again: we must rely on the Lord, because we are not in control.

And so, I thank the Lord each day. He has brought us through trial after trial. He has shown me that dependence on Him is the ultimate connection, the only one that will carry us through. And it can carry you through, too.

Chapter Ten
The New Normal and One Hiccup

I can do all this through him who gives me strength

Philippians 4:13 [25]

Arrival at Palmer and a New Test

Takodah arrived at Palmer Correctional Center, a sentenced facility, on Saturday, April 26. It had been four long weeks since sentencing in Fairbanks, weeks filled with uncertainty and fear after threats to his safety. We didn't know if he would return to TLC or be sent straight to Palmer. When the call came, we were relieved—finally, we could settle into a new chapter.

We scheduled our first visit for Tuesday, April 29. But on Monday, April 28, everything changed again. A correctional officer (CO) pulled Takodah aside at lunch and told him he was still listed under protective custody.

Even though he had signed a waiver saying he felt safe in general population, the paperwork hadn't been cleared. He was taken back to segregation.

What was supposed to be a joyful first week became another waiting game in isolation.

Segregation: A Test of Patience

For nine days, Takodah waited in segregation. Visits were through the glass, just like the earliest days in Anchorage. On May 6, by what I believe was God's will, we had a one-on-one visit: no other visitors, no distractions. I could ask questions, and we could talk more deeply about everything that had happened.

Takodah later told me those nine days tested his patience. He prayed every day for release, but it wasn't until he let go of control that peace came. Another test, another lesson, another moment of transformation.

On May 7, he was finally released into House 6—the faith mod—where he was reunited with brothers from TLC. For their privacy, names have been changed. His mentor, Damion, was there, along with Luke and Bert, welcoming him back. Since then, he has continued growing as a disciple of Christ, and he now works as a cook, starting shifts at 4:00 a.m.

Delays and setbacks will come, even after sentencing. Encourage your loved one to look for meaning in the waiting, and to lean on faith when patience runs out.

When your loved one is sentenced and arrives at their long-term prison facility, life feels both the same and different from the pre-sentencing days. The routines are new, the pace is different, and the reality that this is long-term sinks in. This is the new normal.

Phone Calls

Phone calls are still limited to fifteen minutes, but now more inmates are waiting for their turn. My son says it feels like being at the DMV—you take a number and wait until it's called. In some federal prisons, as my friend Rhonda told me, inmates are allotted a certain number of minutes per month, and they have to keep careful track.

Phone calls are precious. Expect limits, expect waiting, and encourage your loved one to plan wisely.

Visits

Visits in prison (the post-sentencing facility) look similar to those in jail (the pre-sentencing facility), but with some meaningful differences. At my son's prison, you must call at least twenty-four hours in advance to schedule. You can pre-schedule up to a month. If you're driving in from far away—as we often do in Alaska—you can request a two-hour visit, though it's up to the superintendent to approve.

At his prison, visits are held at long tables separated by three-inch plastic dividers. Four inmates may sit at a table, with up to three visitors each. The most significant change: we can hug. At the beginning and end of every visit, you're allowed to lean over the divider and give a hug. After years of glass separating us, that moment of human touch is beyond words. We can even take photos together, with arms around each other's shoulders. That kind of connection—mother and son, side by side—means everything.

If your facility allows it, treasure the physical touch. A hug may be brief, but it can carry you through the longest week.

Weekly Routine

I still visit every Tuesday. Evening visits make for long nights, but I've built a rhythm. I leave home at 4:00 p.m., pick up a dear friend who is visiting her husband, and we arrive by 5:45. My friend often makes dinner, and we have a picnic in the car while waiting for the transport van.

When the van arrives, we sign in, get checked by the CO, and ride the short distance to the campus. Inside, doors open one by one until at last you see your loved one waiting on the other side.

At this facility, maximum security is divided into ten separate houses, each with forty rooms holding bunk beds—up to eighty men per house. They are free to leave their house from 7 a.m. until 10 p.m., but only within the yard. If they are caught in another house, they risk segregation, "the hole."

What struck my son most was the sky. After nearly two years in TLC with only a skylight overhead, he said he had forgotten how vast the sky could feel.

Freedom looks different behind bars, but it still matters. Remind your loved one—and yourself—to notice small freedoms, like seeing the sky.

Serving Others

I now help my son's mentor's mom by driving her to prison every other Sunday. She doesn't like highway driving, so I've taken it on. It feels rewarding to use my love of driving to keep families connected.

Serving others in similar situations not only helps them, but it also strengthens you.

Reflection: Returning With the Gift

Looking back, I see where this journey began—those first days of shock, confusion, and fear. I didn't know how I would survive it. But I have learned that even in prison visits, through glass or across a table, love endures. I have learned that healing does not come all at once, but step by step, through waiting, through faith, through connection.

I pray that you lean on Jesus for strength. Remember the words of Scripture: May the God of hope fill you with all joy and peace as you trust in him, so that you may overflow with hope by the power of the Holy Spirit. —Romans 15:13 [26]

This is the gift I can now offer: connection is possible, healing is possible, hope is possible—even here.

This is our new normal. It is not easy, but it is enough. Each day, I choose to keep walking—connected to my son, to others, and to God.

EPILOGUE: A WORD TO YOU

And now, dear parents walking this road, I hand this gift to you. You may feel overwhelmed, afraid, or even broken, but you are not alone. The path will test you, but it will also shape you. Connection can be sustained. Love can deepen. Hope can rise again.

Take what you need from my story, leave the rest, and know that you, too, can keep walking—one day at a time, one visit at a time, one prayer at a time.

Scripture and References

Introduction

1. The Lord is close to the brokenhearted and saves those who are crushed in spirit. (Psalm 34:18)

2. "For I know the plans I have for you," declares the Lord, "plans to prosper you and not to harm you, plans to give you hope and a future." (Jeremiah 29:11)

Chapter 1: Connection

3. The Father of compassion and the God of comfort, 4 who comforts us in all our troubles, so that we can comfort those in any trouble with the comfort we ourselves receive from God. (2 Corinthians 1:3–4)

Chapter 2: Shock

4. The Lord is close to the brokenhearted and saves those who are crushed in spirit. (Psalm 34:18)

Chapter 3: What You Need to Know Once In Jail

5. Nevertheless, the one who receives instruction in the word should share all good things with their instructor... Let us not become weary in doing good, for at the proper time we will reap a harvest if we do not give up. Therefore, as we have opportunity, let us do good to all people, especially to those who belong to the family of believers. (Galatians 6:6, 9–10)

6. VINE (Victim Information and Notification Everyday) website: https://vinelink.com

7. Securus website: https://securustech.net/

Chapter 4: A New Jail, A New Reality

8. I am not saying this because I am in need, for I have learned to be content whatever the circumstances. I know what it is to be in need, and I know what it is to have plenty. I have learned the secret of being content in any and every situation, whether well fed or hungry, whether living in plenty or in want. I can do all this through him who gives me strength. (Philippians 4:11–13)

Chapter 5: Our Faith Walk

9. Those who live according to the flesh have their minds set on what the flesh desires; but those who live in accordance with the Spirit have their minds set on what the Spirit desires. (Romans 8:5)

10. Emmaus Worldwide: https://www.EmmausWorldwide.org

11. Not giving up meeting together, as some are in the habit of doing, but encouraging one another—and all the more as you see the Day approaching. (Hebrews 10:25)

12. God in Prison: https://www.godinprison.com/

13. Therefore go and make disciples of all nations, baptizing them in the name of the Father and of the Son and of the Holy Spirit. (Matthew 28:19)

14. Faith Bible Institute: https://fbiclass.com/

Chapter 6: The Weight We Carry

15. The one who sins is the one who will die. The child will not share the guilt of the parent, nor will the parent share the guilt of the child. The righteousness of the righteous will be credited to them, and the wickedness of the wicked will be charged against them. (Ezekiel 18:20)

16. Darren Hardy, *Hero's Journey* workbook (unpublished course material, 2021), 17, 19.

17. "Honor your father and mother"—which is the first commandment with a promise—"so that it may go well with you and that you may enjoy long life on the earth." (Ephesians 6:2–3)

Chapter 7: The Early Transfer

18. Trust in the Lord with all your heart and lean not on your own understanding; in all your ways submit to him, and he will make your paths straight. (Proverbs 3:5–6)

19. My dear brothers and sisters, take note of this: Everyone should be quick to listen, slow to speak and slow to become angry. (James 1:19)

Chapter 8: Sentencing

20. Do not be deceived: God cannot be mocked. A man reaps what he sows. (Galatians 6:7)

Chapter 9: The Hit

21. Consider it pure joy, my brothers and sisters, whenever you face trials of many kinds, because you know that the testing of your faith produces perseverance. Let perseverance finish its work so that you may be mature and complete, not lacking anything. (James 1:2–4)

22. The Lord is compassionate and gracious, slow to anger, abounding in love. (Psalm 103:8)

23. Can any one of you by worrying add a single hour to your life? (Matthew 6:27)

24. Be strong and courageous. Do not be afraid or terrified because of them, for the Lord your God goes with you; he will never leave you nor forsake you. (Deuteronomy 31:6)

Chapter 10: The New Normal and One Hiccup

25. I can do all this through him who gives me strength. (Philippians 4:13)

26. May the God of hope fill you with all joy and peace as you trust in him, so that you may overflow with hope by the power of the Holy Spirit. (Romans 15:13)

www.ingramcontent.com/pod-product-compliance
Lightning Source LLC
Chambersburg PA
CBHW020541080526
44583CB00013B/932